ADVANCE PRAISE

"David's thoughtful and incisive editing work, including deep thematic and structural guidance lifted my manuscript from a teetering new draft to a polished, well-developed one. David is the perfect editor who lasers in on areas that need clarification and development, but is also respectful of the author's intentions. He's encouraging and supportive, and also knows how to get the author to be her best self for her best work."

SANDRA HUNTER, recipient of the 2018 Lorian Hemingway Short Story Competition, 2017 Leapfrog Press Fiction Award, 2016 Gold Line Press Chapbook Prize, and three Pushcart nominations; 2018 Hawthornden Fellow and the 2017 Charlotte Sheedy Fellow at the MacDowell Colony; author of *Trip Wires*, *Small Change*, and *Losing Touch*

"I wholeheartedly recommend David Rocklin's editorial services. He provides deep thematic and structural feedback on your process and gives valuable direction to your efforts. His compassionate guidance on how your work communicates to the reader is vital to both beginning and seasoned writers alike. Regardless of the length and scope of your project, David is always ready with encouragement and support through every step of the writing process. He is a master of community building in the literary scene and helps you network with people and agencies to get your words into the right publications and spaces. Engaging this talented coach is a worthy investment in yourself and your literary career."

ARUNI WIJESINGHE, author of *2 Revere Place*, Pushcart nominee

"I found a lot of value in David's editorial services. The written feedback he delivered was thorough and insightful. When we talked about my manuscript over the phone it was clear he'd read it closely and cared about the characters. Rather than giving me prescriptive advice, David asked smart questions and made keen observations that helped me gain new insight into my work."

ALEXANDRA CARMICHAEL, editorial client

"David Rocklin takes you by the hand and travels with you into your work. With his no nonsense approaches and his calming voice will help you hone your work and make it the best it can be."
KATE MARUYAMA, author of *Harrowgate, Family Solstice*

"Writers and writing instructors are in for a treat as they move through the chapters of David Rocklin's excellent new craft book. His gentle, encouraging instruction will motivate writers to open up creatively and get words on the page. His wise, well-crafted exercises and knowledgeable advice about numerous aspects of craft will support teachers in inspiring their students. I highly recommend *The Write Formula* and will be using it myself."
TONI ANN JOHNSON, Flannery O'Connor Award-winning author of *Light Skin Gone to Waste*

THE
WRITE
FORMULA

12 Weeks from Concept
to Completion

DAVID ROCKLIN

ADLER PRESS

To my love, partner, and best friend Nina, for believing in me all these years and without whom this book would not be possible, and to my amazing daughters Ariel and Kavanna, who write their proud, strong, fierce, and courageous stories each and every day. I love you all.

ADLER PRESS
Published by Adler Press
Los Angeles, Calif.

© 2023 David Rocklin

Design by Amanda Wilson
Illustration © Pimpay/iStockphoto.com

Library of Congress Control Number: 2023902658

All rights reserved. No part of this document may be reproduced in any form or by any electronic or mechanical means including information storage and retrieval systems without written permission from the publisher and/or David Rocklin, except by a reviewer who may quote passages in a review.

ISBN 978-1-7339946-4-4 (paperback)

ISBN 978-1-7339946-5-1 (e-book)

CONTENTS

Introduction **vii**

Chapter 1: STORY IDEAS GENERATOR **1**

Chapter 2: THE STORY BUILDING METHOD **11**

Chapter 3: THE STORY STRUCTURE FRAMEWORK **21**

Chapter 4: THE POINT OF VIEW GUIDE **33**

Chapter 5: THE CHARACTER IDENTIFIERS **41**

Chapter 6: THE CHARACTER DEVELOPMENT FORMULA **47**

Chapter 7: THE STORY MOMENTUM GENERATOR **57**

Chapter 8: THE MEMORABLE SETTING CREATOR **63**

Chapter 9: THE SCENE CREATING ROADMAP **71**

Chapter 10: THE PLOT BLUEPRINT **77**

Chapter 11: THE WRITER'S BLOCK DISRUPTORS **83**

Chapter 12: REWRITE SECRETS **95**

A NOTE ON MEMOIR **113**

NOTES ON CRITICISM & REJECTION **117**

CONCLUSION **125**

Acknowledgments **127**

About the Author **129**

INTRODUCTION

How long have you been thinking about starting that novel, short story, or memoir? How long has the idea of writing been with you, but you've not quite been able to bring yourself to sit down and *write*?

Maybe you don't know what to write about. Maybe it's been really hard to figure out how or where to start, how to finish, or how to fill up all those pages in between. I know those feelings well, and I know how easy it is for those feelings to lead to putting things off, and then feeling guilty.

The whole concept of writing a story of any length, from beginning to end, can seem daunting when all you see before you is that empty page. It can feel like the act of writing, even the identity of "writer," is out of reach.

I'm here to tell you it isn't.

I'm going to show you the steps I've followed, from generating an idea to revising a completed story. I've broken it down to a structure that's easy to understand, so you'll always know where you are in the process and what's to come. Each section of this book addresses a concept that you'll use in building your story, no matter the type or length. There are also some exercises in each section to get you going.

Oh, I see that worried look on your face, but don't be nervous! They're fun exercises, I promise. They're designed to get you thinking about your story in ways you may not expect. Ultimately, your writing grows stronger as you become better acquainted with the people and places you're writing about.

This book will help you get where you want to go.

Just where is it that we're going, you ask? Great question—here's where:

- Generating story ideas
- Research
- Story structure
- Point of view
- Character arcs and development
- Conflict

- Setting
- Outlining your story
- Common issues (flashback placement, writer's block)
- Revision
- A word about memoir
- Dealing with criticism and rejection

Seems like a lot but I'm going to break it down for you. We'll go through it step-by-step, together. Now, there are a lot of paths you can take on your way to writing. I want to share the approach that's worked for me. I'm here to help you navigate the often-intimidating journey that is generating an idea, beginning your story, building it out and finishing it. It's the path I've followed and a mission I'm passionate about: helping other writers. I've been fortunate to experience the sensation of putting my work out there and hearing from readers who made a home for my novels. I want to help you experience it too. There's a real joy in finally seeing something you created as a finished, polished piece. There's also the feeling of finally doing that thing you've been dreaming of doing but were perhaps afraid of trying. Maybe it's because no one helped you or believed in you.

I get it, and I want you to reach your goal. I love helping other writers (yes, that means you!) because I've been where you may be now. When I considered starting, what came to mind first wasn't ideas or characters. I dwelled on the reasons not to start. Rejection, the sheer dedication of time, the isolation (at its heart, writing is essentially a solo activity that tends to take us away from other things), the prospect of *how do I fill hundreds of pages??*

But perhaps above all, I didn't know how to get started, or what to do after the first sentence, or the next…

I don't have an MFA. I have a BA in English, which prepares you to write the way that throwing the occasional air jab prepares you to square off with Bruce Lee. And yet, I've completed two novels of literary fiction, both of which have been published. I founded and still host a nine-years-running reading series in Los Angeles. I'm a part of a writers community that I treasure. That didn't come from a formal program (though if you have geographic and financial access, by all means take advantage of it. It's a great way to meet other writers in addition to learning your craft). It came from reading, writing, rewriting, and living.

My journey started as so many writer journeys do. Someone said they believed in me. That was my elementary school teacher, Gloria Luxenberg. I'm privileged to remain in contact with her to this day; she's mentioned in the acknowledgements of each novel I write. After school one afternoon, she assigned me an extra story to read, "The Lottery" by Shirley Jackson. It had the effect on me that she intended. It dazzled and mystified me, that a simple story of people in a small town could turn so sharply, be so subversive and *dangerous*. I came back the following day with questions, all centering on the very thing we'll spend most of our time on in this book: how did the writer do it?

Mrs. Luxenberg didn't have an answer. She had a suggestion, a very important one to follow if you want to be a writer: READ. A LOT. She also told me, "I'll see your name in print one day."

One of the proudest moments of my life was sending her a copy of my debut novel. I know there's someone in your life whom you want to send your writing to, to show them that you *did* it.

As an adult, I participated in a writing workshop. I came armed with a rough draft of a novel and met my second, extraordinarily important influence, my friend and mentor, Susan Taylor Chehak. If Mrs. Luxenberg made me feel like I could do it, Susan made me feel like I could learn *how* to do it. The road was locatable. The tools were there to be acquired.

It took several failed attempts at novels (if you ask, I'll happily regale you with my 1,000+ page attempt at horror, the jumping off point being Passover—I'm not kidding) and a lot of rejections from agents and editors to arrive, finally, at a novel worthy of publication. I wandered, got good and lost, found my way again, made lots of missteps, threw a metric ton of material away—repeatedly—and grew frustrated. I sent things out and received rejections both encouraging and, well, not so much (we'll talk about rejection too). But I never stopped writing, and over the time I *thought* I was spending in pursuit of the impossible dream of creating something good enough to be published, I was also accomplishing a different, but deeply related, goal. I was getting better even as I was getting lost. I was learning what writing a novel truly involved: an idea, a plan (even a rough, vague one), a certain degree of relentlessness, and someone to guide you and cheer you on.

I'm here to help you with all of those. Ready?

Let's get after it.

Chapter One

STORY IDEAS GENERATOR

HOW DO YOU START TO WRITE SOMETHING IF YOU AREN'T SURE WHAT THAT SOMETHING IS?

You'd like to write a novel, or perhaps a short story, or maybe a memoir, or some flash fiction, but you don't really have an idea of what you'd like to write. You just know you want to. You HAVE to.

Or maybe you do have a germ of an idea. An inkling about where it will be set, or when, or who it will (maybe) be about. Nothing specific, nothing detailed enough that you can foresee all the events, but you have a fuzzy sense of it. You just can't quite think of the right opening, or the next thing, and the one after that. So now what?

Before a fighter steps into the ring, before a musician plays the first note, they warm up. They get a little loose. Warming up in the writing sense not only gets you ready for the task at hand. It starts all the wheels in your writer mind turning. Warming up generates ideas.

Let's talk about generating those idea possibilities.

1. FREEWRITING

Freewriting is just what the name implies. No structure, no outline, no thought as to where to start or stop. It's writing in an unpremeditated way. All you need is the notion that's in your head as you read this. I bet you can think of at least one that's just been hanging around in there. As other random thoughts come and go from moment to moment, that one's always sticking around, right?

I call this the flystrip effect. Every day we're bombarded with thoughts, ideas, remembered fragments of dreams or old memories, and perhaps we think, "That one might make a good story." And then it's gone as the events and responsibilities of the day wash it down the mental drain. Don't spend too much time chasing those. Instead, pay attention to the ones that stick to you like flies to flystrips. The ones that twenty-four or forty-eight hours later, are still hanging on to you. Those may be clinging to you for a reason.

Perhaps you've no ideas at all. That's perfectly ok—freewriting can generate them. Put away your laptop, pad and pen, or whatever you like to write with. Take a walk. Take a drive. Now, go back to those writing tools and with each step, ask yourself: *What am I thinking of? What image is in my thoughts right now?* Hey, if the only thing you come up with is "I have zero ideas," there's your idea. *I have zero ideas right now, because all I can think of is…* Again, freewriting is writing with no pressure on yourself. Something will happen when you sit down, set a timer for 20-30 minutes, and just start with anything. *Anything* leads to the next anything, and the next, and when the timer goes off, you may have generated one word, one sentence, that in turn clings to you over the next twenty-four hours. And that may be your key to unlock what it is you want to write about and how you might approach it.

> **FREEWRITING EXERCISE:** Grab the first idea that comes to you, or the last one on your mind when you went to bed last night. Set a timer for thirty minutes and just write without a care as to what you're saying, how you're saying it, or who might ever see it.

2. PROMPTS

I mentioned that I created a reading series that's been running in Los Angeles for nine years now. During each show, we play a fun game called Live Write. The audience members each create a secret prompt of some kind. It can be a random thought, a belief, a question, a situation, a song snippet, or a line of dialogue from their favorite movie. I choose one of them, and two volunteers from the audience have about ten minutes to write something on the spot, based on that prompt. Then they read what they wrote to the audience, and everyone votes on the piece they like best. The "winner" comes back the following month as a featured reader at the next show.

Writers can easily spend weeks laboring over one sentence. For us, the concept of just writing on the fly with only the barest of ideas to hang it all on can be intimidating. But everyone who's ever participated tells me after that they got a lot out of it. Some of them went on to expand what they wrote into full pieces, and some of those got published.

Here's how you can do it:

Set a timer for 10-15 minutes (or longer if you're feeling it) around a prompt. Prompts are all around you! Grab the first headline you see on the news. Steal the subject line from one of your emails. Open a book to a random page, and write around the first sentence you read. Ask your friends to send you a sentence about anything at all, and write around that.

Here are some prompt ideas you can use to get started:

- Create a character with personality traits of someone you love, but the physical characteristics of someone you don't care for (or even hate—better yet!). How do they turn out when you write about them? How does blending those traits together make you feel about them? Why?
- Eavesdrop on a random conversation and turn it into a love story, no matter how badly you need to twist things to fit. How much did you have to twist? Why?
- Choose four random words from the dictionary, then write a story using all of them. Why did it come out that way?
- You or your character receives an unexpected text: "Can two people be together too long?" Who is it from? What do they mean? Why did they send it to you/your character?

EXERCISE: THE YELLOW LIGHT GAME
You or your character are in a car (notice that I didn't say whether you/they are driving or a passenger. Those details are up to you). The car is approaching a lighted intersection when the light turns yellow. What happens? Do you/your character slow down in anticipation of the red light? Speed up to get through? Why? Is this a chase? Is someone late, and for what? Is someone else in the car, saying what needs to happen? Why? Are they injured and in need of a doctor? Are they having an emotional breakdown? Why? Are you/your character helping them get away from the reason for that breakdown (abusive relationship, etc.)? Why did you/your character help them? Why did they turn to you? Happenstance, or something more? A connection? What is the backdrop of this situation? Be as expansive and imaginative as you want.

Did you notice a common thread through these prompt suggestions? The most important question a writer can ask of the material is *why*. *Why* leads down multiple avenues. It unlocks possibilities. Ask it, and ask it often, as you think about the various components of your piece. It's an extraordinarily important and revealing word when wielded by a writer!

You'll see a lot of *whys* throughout this program.

3. PASS IT!

EXERCISE: Story creation lightning round

In this exercise, ask and answer basic questions as fast as you can (ten seconds or less), then pass it to the next person. You can do this with a couple other people, or a whole bunch of people. You can do this alone as well, though the spontaneity of someone throwing unexpected twists into the exercise really makes it fun. You don't need to find another writer for this one. Anyone will do!

First person: Who is the character (physical attributes, emotional state, anything you think might be relevant)?...PASS!

Second: Where are they (time/place)?...PASS!

Third: At the moment the story opens, where are they in terms of story. What's happening?...PASS!

Fourth: What's their conflict/problem?...PASS!

Fifth: Make their problem worse...PASS!

Sixth: Make their problem even worse...PASS!

Seventh: Make it WAY worse...PASS!

Last: FIX IT

What just happened? You created some flash fiction, that's what! No adhering to an outline because you feel like you have to. Free thinking and writing. You let the character and the choices they'd make—based upon who they are and what's happening around them—dictate plot, conflict, and resolution.

Know what else happened? You just made your first revision! By changing the dynamics and introducing new and unexpected elements to something that already existed, you revised story in terms of tone and direction. Congrats!

As you try out these exercises, you'll also be trying out the ideas they generate. It's a bit like trying on clothes, right? You're moving from one thing to the next, looking for the one that feels right. You may try on one, two, or a lot. As you move from idea to idea, you may feel a bit overwhelmed. Which idea is the "right" one to write about?

An agent I met once at a writers' conference said something that remains with me whenever I think about what I might want to write. "What kind of story is it? I mean, you're asking readers to spend a lot of time there."

As writers, we're asking our readership to set aside time over a period of days, weeks, perhaps months, depending on their reading pace (and, let's face it, our ability to immerse and involve them in what we've written). Taken at face value, this is an intimidating sentiment.

Think about it this way: you're going to spend a lot more time in and with your story than your readers will. Months, at a bare minimum, if it's a short story, and if it's a novel or memoir, it'll most likely be well in excess of a year, probably closer to two if we factor in revisions.

> "The most important question a writer can ask of the material is *why*."

I don't say that to intimidate you. Rather, let me suggest you approach your story idea not from the standpoint of "what does the reader want," but what do *you*, the writer, want. You should write, first and foremost, for yourself.

You can try to write to the current popular trend in publishing, but by the time you have a draft ready to be seen, that trend will be over. You can try to anticipate the next trend, and maybe you'll even guess right. But is that why you're yearning to write? Is that why you're willing to devote the next year or more creating something that doesn't exist yet? Will writing to a trend keep you dedicated, relentless, and determined to make this happen? It wouldn't for me.

Let me ask you this:

Wouldn't you rather write something that you'd love to read if you came across it at your local bookshop or online? Wouldn't you rather write that unrealized (but not for long!) seed of a thing that you find yourself dwelling on during work calls, thinking about at night, jotting the occasional note about?

That thing is why you're here. Now let's talk about where we can go together to find it.

Maybe that thing is tied to a particular period in your life. A long-ago, as-yet-unresolved event, or one of those moments you always fantasize about going back to because now you know exactly how to deal with it. Maybe it's tied to a period in world history. Maybe it hasn't happened yet; you can't stop thinking about a future or an alternative time that you want to create. Perhaps it's a person that you've been thinking about. A real person, or a composite of people, or maybe you've been imagining yourself into a scenario that's never happened before, to you or anyone else.

The story we're going to generate, plot out, write, and revise together should come from you choosing the story you want to spend time with.

For me—and maybe, for you—the story comes from a picture that finds me and won't leave (hello, flystrip effect!). I begin with what I see in that image. Is there a person? Where is the place they're in located? Why are they staring that way? What's going on through that window behind them? Was there someone else with them in the moment before? Is someone about to show up, or is something about to happen that will change this moment, perhaps forever?

In other words, I ask a lot of '*whys*'.

Whether the image is something fixed and real, or something in my memory, or something that never was (but now has taken up residence with me and may as well have happened), I look first for what I know is there. Then I start to imagine my way into the gaps between what I can see, what I can demonstrate, and what I don't know. Writing in almost any genre, be it fiction, memoir, short story or even poetry, is speculating on the gaps between what we know and what we don't know about a particular person, moment, or event. The thing you can see sparks the desire to write, but all the things that can't be seen—how people felt, what they said, what they did, all that has been hidden away by the passing years or simply by the fact that you haven't written your way to them yet—that's what happens when you're provoked towards the possible.

Whether you choose the world, or whether the world chooses you, when you come to an idea, ask yourself if it's something you're excited about exploring. That excitement will translate to the reader. They'll see, in what you write, the reason why you burned to write it. And that's a book people will want to read.

Speaking of reading, read. A LOT.

"If you want to be a writer, you must do two things above all others. You must read a lot and you must write a lot." That particular quote belongs to Stephen King, but the sentiment is one you'll hear from every writer who's serious about it. Reading is integral to writing, and the reason is simple.

You learn in order to do, and you do in order to do well.

What do I mean by that?

Anyone who wants to learn how to do something begins by observing others who already know how to do it. The new kid at school watches the other kids in class, at lunch, and at recess. She watches those who know how to do what she wants to do. She gravitates to them, and she learns. A first-time student of martial arts watches classes, or movies, and gradually moves toward a system that draws her. A grown man who never learned to swim watches swimmers, finds a style he thinks he might be able to do, learns about it, and eventually gets into the water.

In the end, the observer discovers what they're interested in learning to do. They try to do it, fail, do it again, and fail bigger and better, to hat-tip Samuel Beckett. In the way that there's no substitute for experience, there's no substitute for observing the experience you want to try or for the process of learning about it and being drawn to it. That magnetic draw toward what you want to do is the very same energy source you'll rely on to keep you from quitting when you fail.

You've come to the decision to write. Now it's time to rediscover the experience of reading. Because it won't be the same as before. Not for you.

Why?

Don't worry—reading for the pure, transportive pleasure of it will never go away. It will be enhanced (I would even say, improved) by all you'll be getting from it when you read like a writer.

Some reading suggestions:
READ IN YOUR GENRE
Want to write Afrofuturistic fiction? Period romance? Literary fiction set in the past (hey, I know a writer you should read...)? Crime? Horror? Story collections centered on fractured families? LGBTQIA? Then you should read the work of those mining similar veins to yours. See what stories they found. See what they did with them.

READ OUTSIDE YOUR GENRE
There's a commonly held belief about genre fiction (thriller, mystery, romance) that it's plot-driven, paced to move swiftly, but poorly or simply written. Similarly, there's a belief about literary fiction that it's beautifully phrased, but just floats around with no sense of narrative drive.

Neither of these is entirely true; there are genre writers whose work is as beautifully written as anything you'll encounter, and literary writers whose stories are incredibly compelling. The key is there's a lot to learn from any writer whose work has been published.

READ TO SEE HOW THEY DID IT

The deeper and wider you read, the more familiar you'll become with the tools, techniques, brushes, and canvases writers employ to create their worlds. As I mentioned at the outset, I didn't have easy access to graduate studies in writing, nor did I have mentors or a circle of writers from whom to learn the most important lesson I needed in order to realize my dream of writing and publishing a novel: how do writers do it?

This touches upon one of the most critical phases of writing, whether a first draft or the umpteenth revision: your outline. We'll spend a good deal of time on outlines, and you'll hear me say more than once, your outline isn't meant to bind you inescapably. It's a map in the adventurous sense of the word. It's guidance, but within it lies permission to stray from it if and when the characters demand it.

There's an approach I employ when reading, that we'll get into in the Outline section. I call it the Blueprint Method. It's a way of simultaneously deepening your reading experience and unlocking this very question: how'd they do it?

There's another important benefit to reading this way:

READ TO SEE THAT YOU CAN DO IT

Not *if* you can. THAT you can. You *can* write a novel, or a memoir, or a short story. Like anything, it'll take practice, diligence, and dedication. You need to get comfortable with the process of trying, failing, and trying again. But guess what? If you've come this far, if you've done what we've covered to this point, **you already started writing.**

Let's acknowledge something, writer to writer. We all experience feelings of envy or inadequacy. You know that doubting voice. The one that whispers, "*I can't do that. Only they can.*" Make friends with those feelings, because they never truly go away. Each time I start a new novel, I have them. My writer friends and colleagues, published or not, have them. It's absolutely ok to have them. Just don't let them stop you.

Those feelings may be sparked when you read another writer. But stay with me on this: if you do this exercise, and the others we'll talk about, enough, you'll feel a shift in how you see yourself and your work. You'll begin to realize that this thing isn't beyond your grasp. You'll start feeling more comfortable with the tools of writing. You'll go back over the books you read, and you'll find yourself thinking, *Maybe I would have made a different choice here.* That doesn't mean you'll feel you're better or they're worse. You'll be developing your own take on how, among the myriad ways a story can be told over the course of thousands of words, you'd do it. You're finding your unique voice.

HERE'S AN EXERCISE TO SUM THIS UP: What's something that stays with you? Something that makes you feel angry, sad, grateful, lustful, or afraid, whenever you think about it? Say what it is, then why it has that effect on you. Write it down.

Chapter Two

THE STORY BUILDING METHOD

AT THIS POINT, WE'VE WARMED UP. We've done some exercises that hopefully generated one or two ideas, or at least illuminated the idea(s) you already have. If you did have an idea, we've started to explore some new perspectives about it. Perhaps it's already started to morph a bit, into a timeframe you didn't consider, or a character that hadn't previously occurred to you.

Most importantly, we've started you on the path to realizing your dream of writing. Together, we're going to finish what you start.

Now you have something of an idea. The setting, the characters, the plot, the end it's all headed toward wait to be found. Somewhere in that idea, the story lives. What now?

My first novel, *The Luminist,* is loosely inspired by a period in the life of Julia Margaret Cameron, an English woman who became involved with photography in its infancy. She was remarkable and unique for her time in that she tenaciously pursued this little-known art and science against all societal pressures and expectations. I saw an installation of her photographs at the Getty Museum in Los Angeles. Now, I'm not a photographer, and I had no previous experience with the country the story is set in, but something about those images really captured me, as did a quote on the wall of the Getty next to her first ever photograph: "I longed to arrest all beauty that came before me."

It had me right then and there. This obsession of hers, to take a moment out of the world and hold it still, became the reason I knew I had to write it. Eventually, it became the novel's heart. The photographs themselves, the way she depicted close faces half-bathed in shadow, reflected her own life as she fought to emerge from the shadow of a culture that held her back. The fact that she lost a child at birth, pre-photography, meant that the only way she had to hold on to her child's memory was that most fragile of things: memory itself. Out of a simple visit to a museum, a vivid, breathing character came and with her a story that became a novel.

What do you do with your idea? You build on it.

Doing research for your story isn't a one-time thing. For my second novel, *The Night Language*, I researched before I started writing the first draft in order to immerse myself in the time period (England and Abyssinia from the mid-1800s on to the dawn of the 20th century). As I wrote that draft, I conducted research on story elements that came up that I didn't know the answer to. What would a poor man eat for lunch? Where would someone who wasn't accepted by society, and who didn't want to be known or noticed, live in Paris? What epithets were used against people of color in England at that time? How long would it take, and by what mode of transportation, to cross the Channel to London?

Often, what I found while researching bumped my story in an unexpected direction. Research into where the main character might live in Paris, for example, led to the creation of a new, and as it turns out, popular, supporting character. Similarly, research about a sea voyage from Abyssinia to England during a subsequent draft resulted in a profound, substantial change in the story, from an unlikely father figure to the love of the main character's life.

Research at the very beginning of your process, before you even have a sense of what your story is or who your characters are, allows you to learn about your story's world. Through that research, you'll also begin to shape your sense of the people who will populate that world. The more you read on the broad, general topics or themes you think you want to write about, you'll find that your research becomes more and more focused. It narrows as you develop your ideas. It will also branch out into different areas. You may want to write a crime thriller, and so you begin to research the most notorious heists in history. Your research may take you into the tools of the trade. You may find yourself looking for information on how banks mark bills. That may lead you to ask, "Is that exploding dye really purple? What's it made from? Is it true that it won't wash out?"

Then you look into the laws of other countries. Which ones won't extradite? Which ones have confidential banking laws? Where do criminals go to launder their money? What exactly is a fence? If the main character pulled off their dream heist, where would they go to hide? To spend it all? Who was the money really for?

See how asking questions leads to new ideas?

The more you delve, the more you find yourself creating. Your research into the banking laws of Switzerland, for example, might lead to you creating a character who works at a bank. We'll get into this more as we examine plot and character arcs, but supporting characters often come into being because they possess a skill or a trait that the main character doesn't have but the story needs, such as a character who knows the ins and outs of a bank.

Once you start writing, you'll quite likely go back to your research as new questions arise. That's great! Researching with a developing sense of your story and the characters who populate it allows you to be focused and strategic in mining sources for information that will lend authenticity.

Authenticity is, in the end, a large part of what you're after. Your research should be designed not only to educate yourself in the story's large themes and small details. It should also give that story an air of truth. Katherine Boo, author of *Behind the Beautiful Forevers: Life, Death and Hope in a Mumbai Undercity* (a remarkable work of empathetic, clear-eyed journalism) speaks of "the earned fact." In order to write about something, you want to experience it as much as possible, so it reads in an authentic way. I like to immerse myself in the world I'm writing about, despite the fact that I might not be able to physically put myself there. My current novel-in-progress is set in Germany just before the end of the 19th century and spans a period of time to the opening of the first camps. While I would dearly love to travel, the pandemic (at the time of this writing) makes that impossible. Moreover, much of what I'm writing about no longer exists in the places I would want to see. And yet, I can still immerse myself to the degree that I need; for me, I'm not ready to write until what I'm writing about feels less like a story I've made up and more like a memory of something that actually happened to me. That's how immersed I need to be.

So, if you can't go to the place(s) you're writing about (too far, too expensive, they don't actually exist), how do you "earn the facts" you're creating? How do you become intimately familiar with your world?

In a word: research!

To be sure, research is critical to your writing whether you can travel to the site of the story or not. You may be writing about a place or a person you know intimately, but there are backstories and secondary characters, and in order to get to know them all well enough, you want to be able to readily answer your story's questions about them. What would they do in a situation like this? What would they say, and (don't forget) *why?* Is it because they're living below the poverty line (research: what was the average income in that year)? Is it because English isn't their first language (research: would someone from Ghana understand or use American slang circa 1985, and what words might not have a counterpart in their language)? Is it because they went through a horrible breakup and they're highly distrustful (research: what subtle signs of PTSD might someone their age or demographic display)?

You may run into rich veins of research opportunities before you start, during your writing, or in your revision. Most likely, all three, and more than once. That's just as it should be! The only limit there is to the types of research you can use is your own imagination. Of course, you want to stick to established sources and avoid crowd-sourced sites.

Research is not just the process of finding out about something. It's also about how it *feels*. You can read articles describing what happens to the human body when you get punched right in the solar plexus. It's an altogether different thing to experience it, to see how it feels, to understand what happens to your breathing and vision, not to mention the panic or the anger. To fight for your next gulp of air.

Not that I'm suggesting you ask your friend or partner to haul off and hit you. But on-the-ground, tactile experience is an extremely valid form of research when it's available.

The research you do now may not make it into your story as a referenced passage or a theme. You may use a little of it, or none of it. But what's the first thing we all do when we travel to a new place and we set our suitcase down? We look around. We take in the new sights and sounds. That's what you're doing with higher-level, general research, which offers fantastic windows into the world your story will inhabit.

A note: no matter how thorough and reputable the source, never rely on only one thing. If you draw all your facts from one source, you may find that you've stopped writing about how a thing was or is. Instead, you're writing about how one person said those things are/were.

Don't neglect works of fiction when it comes to sources of the time you're depicting. Writers working in or about the period you're interested in were looking to interpret, depict, and illuminate that world. You can learn a great deal by taking note of the big and small things they created their stories around. The same goes for the art, music, and poetry of the time. Make the artistic views of the world a part of your research.

Here are some more traditional research resources I've really come to value:

BIG PICTURE RESEARCH

The first resources we often turn to when researching our stories. Big-picture, wide-ranging sweeps of the overall world that your story is a part of.

BOOKS AND MOVIES

When you're looking for a way in to the world you want to write about, nothing beats books. Lots of them. Books about the time, the place, the clothes, the economy, the movies out during that time, the music, the food. Read about the social climate, the political climate, the war(s), the customs, and the day-to-day realities of people at that time. Even if the time is now and the world is the one you live in, immersing yourself into the intimate details may well reveal things big and small that you didn't know. Things that will enrich the world your story inhabits.

Watching a movie about the time, or even better, from the time (if the technology existed) is a wonderful, immediate way to access the emotional aspects of your story idea as you bear witness to the way people moved through a world similar to yours. The details—the way the world was, the way the rooms and the clothes looked, the way people spoke to each other in public and in private.

> Here's a fun, quick exercise to do with a movie from or about your timeframe. Take a scene from it. One that affected you or informed you as you consider your own story. Write a paragraph on how you feel after watching it. Take into account the mood and what aspects of that scene make you feel the way you do.
>
> Now, replay it with the audio off. Watch it in silence. Make note of what's missing. The big, thematic sounds, like dialogue or music, and the small ones, the little touches like the sounds of the street, footsteps, drawn breath. Write that scene again this time using words to add those missing touches in. Describe the car horn, the opening of a door, the ice clinking in a glass.
>
> Did you feel differently watching it this way? More importantly, did you write the scene differently the second time? Congrats! You just did some research, and then used that research to inform your writing. Well done!

We'll touch upon this again when we get to Setting, but you also formed an opinion about the world you wrote. Pretty cool!

DOCUMENTARIES AND PODCASTS

Want to gain some understanding of American racial strife in the jazz age? Look to documentaries, podcasts, and other media of a journalistic type that addresses the subject. The best of these are thoughtfully curated, well organized, and incredibly informative. They can provide any number of avenues you'll want to follow as your research deepens, and can point the way to the details that will help you bring your world alive.

LETTERS AND RECORDS

Ideally, your research should be evocative as well as informative. You want to learn about the backdrop, climate, and particulars of your story, sure. But it's truly special when you find a source that also centers you emotionally in the period, and by extension, in your writing. Among the best sources for this are letters and records from the time/place you're learning about. Universities and foundations devoted to the legacies of prominent individuals or the study of eras in history and the fields of inquiry (science, technology, social dynamics, etc.) making advances at that time are an internet search away and may well have collections that you can request access to. During the research for my first novel, *The Luminist*, I asked for and graciously received access to the photographic archives at the Getty Museum in Los Angeles. Bearing witness to the actual preserved works of other human beings speaking contemporaneously of the world and their place in it is immeasurably valuable and truly evocative.

MAPS OF THE PERIOD

I vividly recall seeing a movie that was filmed on the college campus I attended. A character rode a bicycle down a street I knew well, turned right at an intersection, and was suddenly riding through a setting I knew to be no fewer than ten miles away. That incongruity took me right out of the story, and as good as the movie was, I never found my way back in.

While you can absolutely fictionalize places to suit your story, it never hurts to get your basic facts right. Your character can't walk from Los Angeles to San Francisco in an hour, nor could your historically-set character take a train from New York to Maine if there weren't tracks yet (or trains, for that matter). Remember: places, like people, change over time. Boundaries arise that weren't there before. Territories expand or contract through war, peace, trade, and the fall of empire. Getting yourself grounded in the time and place of your story is immensely important, and maps of the period are not only educational as to where your characters lived, but in what way they lived. Perhaps they lived on a prairie, and based upon that era's map, there were no towns around them. That tells you something about how they had to shape their lives. They needed to be self-sufficient, proficient at farming or raising livestock, hardy and resilient, aware of precious resources like water and where to find it (and how long it would take to reach, what they'd need for the journey to and from, the dangers from animals and other people competing for the same resource…). Or perhaps they were none of those things, and that's one of the main points of your plot: they're up against an unforgiving landscape and lacking the tools to make it.

If your story takes place in a world that doesn't exist, create your own map! Start in the center with a "you are here" pin for your main character. Then, fill in what's immediately around them. Think of your own home as the center of a map of your town or city. What's right next door? What's down the street? Where are the stores, the gym, the businesses? Does your character work near home, or do they have to commute a great distance? And of course, don't forget to ask, as to each map point, *why*. Why does the character go there? Why does the character like it there? Do they long for somewhere else? Why or why not?

You'll find that you're not only creating a reference tool, you're discovering events in your story.

DETAIL RESEARCH
PHOTOS, ART

I'm a pretty visual person. The experience of plunging into an image from another place or time is very inspiring to me. Often, an arresting image leads me to research what I'm seeing, and something in that inquiry strikes against the image and throws sparks. Those sparks become the idea around which a story develops.

It was a photo I found in the Getty archives, while researching my first novel, that generated the idea for the second, *The Night Language*.

In that novel, the main character's name is Alamayou. Alamayou did, in fact, exist, though he was much different than my novel depicted. I found a photo of him as a young boy, newly arrived in London, when I was researching my first novel, *The Luminist,* at the Getty. I couldn't look away from that young boy's haunted face. I had to know more about this child who was taken by force of war from his home in Abyssinia and brought across the world to an unimaginable city: London in the mid-1800s. That was the image; I learned via research that he didn't live past age seventeen in life (I won't say what happens to him in the novel), and he was always a lonely figure. Image and fact collided, and the thrown sparks were this: I wanted to write a life for Alamayou that he didn't get to have in reality. That, of course, meant love (and love isn't worthy of a novel unless it's threatened).

Go get yourself lost in images. Museums, bookstores, photographic exhibits, Instagram accounts that jibe with your idea. Scroll through and see if one doesn't stop you. Spend time with that one, as it may be trying to tell you something.

PRESERVED SITES, INSTALLATIONS, SOCIETIES, AND ORGANIZATIONS DEDICATED TO CULTURAL LEGACY

Like photos or paintings (or music, for that matter), physical spaces can evoke ideas, and inspire the emotions attached to them. Old theaters, homes, historic neighborhoods where people like your characters once lived and died, are all rich resources to bear in mind. Take a walk and talk to the locals. Look at the photos on the walls of the stores, tracing their histories back to the early days of the neighborhood. It's really a fascinating journey.

> **EXERCISE:** What year does your story take place in? Find one movie made or released that year, or one book written that year, or one photograph taken or painting created. Even a song written that year works. Take a deep dive into what's shown, what's said, what's worn, what's done. What have you learned about what was happening that year that might be a cool addition to your story?

Chapter Three

THE STORY STRUCTURE FRAMEWORK

SO, YOU'VE GENERATED AN IDEA. You've begun your research to expand your knowledge and intimacy around that idea. You're beginning to know what you want to write. Let's take a moment and celebrate how far you've come!

But wait...how do you go from the beginning to the end?

Figuring this part out—the structure of the story—can be one of the most challenging aspects of writing. In the next sections, we're going to talk about the basic components of structure: the three-act arc, character arc/development (including conflict), and setting.

At its essence, structure is the frame within which your story is told. It starts and it ends, and between those poles, things happen that lead from one to the other. Sounds pretty simple, right?

Now think about a year in your life. It began, and it ended, and between those poles, things happened. Perhaps a lot of things. Unexpected things. Chaotic, stressful, interminable things (pandemic, anyone?). Blissful, lovely, profound things. Mundane things. And in the end, when you sit and try to take in the year with all its strands and dangling threads, it somehow makes sense that it leads to where you are, even if at the time it felt like a jumble of moments coming at you from every which way.

That year is a lot like your story. Life, when viewed from the inside of each moment, appears disassembled. But when we look back on it from a distance (time, a different location, after an event like a birth, wedding, or passing) it arranges itself chronologically, day to day, week to week. Or it shuffles itself into a thematic collection (ever go back through your mental collection of people you dated, looking for common traits and patterns?). The structure you create to form your story is a bit like a recollection. Living it is one thing, but when we remember, our mind imposes order and a framework around it.

In other words, you can absolutely do this with your story. You do it all the time!

A thought: though we're going to spend some time on story structure here, don't worry that your first draft will feel like a bit of a jumble. That's good! That first draft is where you put everything on the page, and revisions are where the structure will emerge.

THE THREE-ACT STRUCTURE

No matter what sort of story you're writing, it will have a beginning, a middle, and an end. Each of those sections, or acts, is tied to the others, and each is tied as well to one or more plot events that drive the story from one to the next. If you like math, roughly fifty percent of your story will be comprised of the second act, or the middle, of the piece. The remaining fifty percent is divided—not necessarily in an equal or even way—between the beginning and the end.

Over the course of these three acts, your main character(s) will commence and complete their journey. The plot will build to the realization of the character's goal(s). The end will tie things up (or not—did I hear someone say sequel?).

As you approach this phase, don't worry about nailing everything down in a precise way. Much of this emerges as you write, and most of all, as you revise. But it helps to have a rough sense of these aspects:

ACT ONE

The first act of your story establishes the world it occupies and the rules governing your characters. There will be at least some exposition as the reader gets accustomed to the setting and "how things work around here," and there will be shadings of what's waiting around the corner. If the rules are the same or substantially similar to those the readers are familiar with (i.e., your story takes place in the recognizable present or a well-known past here on plain old Earth), there's less to do. If the story is set in another time or a different country, or there are supernatural or extraordinary themes, you'll want to introduce that in the first act.

Think of it like this: Act One should answer these questions: *Where are we? When are we? Who are we?*

By the time this act concludes, the story's world will change. That change is also called a plot point or an inciting incident. It's where your story truly begins. This is a little different than the so-called "hook," which is usually in the first 1% and corresponds to the first interesting thing that's not scene-setting or exposition. It may even be the very first sentence!

The first plot point of a story will generally take place about one-quarter of the way into the story; in other words, at the end of the first act. Something has happened between that initial hook and this inciting event to bump your character into a new situation or issue. It's usually the first truly important event in the story, and will commence the character's true arc (which is, of course, quite different than the life the character thought they were in the process of living) by sending them headlong into the second act. It forces the character to embark on a journey or undertake an action. It pulls them out of their ordinary world, into the main action of the story. The inciting incident can be an attack, or an offer, or a life changing incident. It can be the beginning of a journey or the end of a way of life. It can be the discovery of a secret, a betrayal, a realization, or a crime. It can be whatever your writerly brain cooks up.

> "Act One should answer these questions:
> Where are we, when are we, and who are we."

There should be an emotional, as well as a plot, consequence to the inciting incident, so we care about the character as they embark on this new journey. It should change the character's world, even physically—the character has to go somewhere else physically, mentally, emotionally, or strategically to do what's needed to respond to the conflict raised by this event. That gives your story a chance to refresh, and it broadens the scope of the world you're depicting.

When you think about what your character does after that plot point hits, it's important that there be consequences on *both* sides of the action the character takes. What does this mean?

Action-based stories, thrillers, mysteries, horror, present their story arcs in more explicit terms and offer ready lessons for the study of structure. Let's look at one of my favorite movies, *Jaws*.

We all remember the set-up, right? Coastal village, summer's coming and bringing much needed tourist dollars, massive shark lurking in the water...

Act One introduces us to the film's cast of characters, primarily Chief Brody, oceanologist Matt Hooper, salty fisherman Quint, the mayor and the town council, and of course, the shark (who was named Bruce on the set, after Steven Spielberg's lawyer!). Each character has their needs and goals, be it keeping the peace, generating income over the 4th of July, studying sharks, killing sharks, and hungry Bruce who, like Oliver Twist, just wants some more.

Act One ends, in my mind, with a slap across the face.

Let's unpack a couple of points. First, recall the notion that there needs to be consequences on both sides of the character's arc once the inciting incident hits. Consider this moment in the film: Mrs. Kintner, mother of the second shark victim (a young boy named Alex) approaches Chief Brody and Matt Hooper, along with the town's mayor, just as they're celebrating the capture and killing of what they believe to be the responsible shark. Matt Hooper has just informed Chief Brody that the odds of the hoisted, dead animal being the right one are "a hundred to one."

Bump. That line introduces the arc of the next act, and the consequences on either side of what the characters have to do. The shark is still out there, still a lethal threat. The town's financial fate is still threatened as the beaches need to be closed lest anyone else die. The mayor wants to ignore the danger. And then Mrs. Kintner comes, funeral attire and all, and slaps Brody across the face for not taking action sooner.

The consequences are both external (hunt and kill the shark or be killed, literally and financially) and internal (take action despite the terror, or live with the blood of innocents on the collective hands of those who did nothing). With that, the incident pushes the characters off the path they thought they were following, toward a new, dangerous, unexpected destination.

Another consideration—notice how I phrased the Act One inciting incident in *Jaws*: "Act One ends, *in my mind*, with a slap across the face."

"In my mind?" Isn't there universal agreement on where acts end, or what the inciting incidents are? In a word, no. Some are quite obvious. Others are subtle, so much so that in scanning the structure of a piece, you might consider more than one possibility. Some instructors will say that there are five acts, or seven. And that's perfectly ok! As we've mentioned, and will undoubtedly mention again, your approach to structure is best when it's flexible. Have some thoughts on where the story is headed, certainly, but have openness as well, to what the story may give you in terms of possibilities you didn't think of when you began.

Inciting incidents in fiction, particularly literary or adult fiction, can be harder to recognize. But they're there. Let's look once again at *The Great Gatsby*. At the shoulder of our first-person narrator, Nick Carraway, we step away from the place he knew to a new world of glamour and wealth that he fully realizes he doesn't belong in. He's a romantic at heart and he loves his cousin Daisy despite her callous and vain nature. Just as he finds a place in a line of work that cements his station well below those he's socializing with, a door opens, literally and figuratively. The opening act ends with a party at the next-door estate of Jay Gatsby, and Nick's act of entering that party through the ornate front door immerses him in a luminous corruption that will engulf, inspire, endanger, and ultimately turn away from him in the same way the world Jay Gatsby endured in the name of seeking the ceaseless past turns away from his floating corpse (if that's a spoiler—hey, the novel was published in 1925! I suppose you don't know about that Darth Vader-Luke Skywalker thing either).

The simple act of walking into a party. It's a masterful inciting incident precisely because it's so subtle. It doesn't seem like a red flag to the characters, though the clouds do appear on our reader horizon in the form of Nick's (and Fitzgerald's) narrative voice recalling for us the events of one summer. "The lights grow brighter as the earth lurches away from the sun..."

How about the "both sides" consequence question?

There are clear consequences to Nick walking through that door. The consequences if he doesn't, though less clear, are also there, embedded in Nick's personality. He craves a different life than the one he has. He craves acceptance, and he strives for a romantic ideal that was, in the post-war years of the Jazz Age, woven into the fabric of a country newly emerged from a terrible global conflict, eager to put the past behind it (and with it the vestiges of the war, the crippled and wounded, the lost souls). Against this backdrop, how lovely this writing is, that presents a man seeking to reshape his future self alongside a man trying to recapture the great love of his past, and we the readers witness the failure of both men. Nick risks losing his chance to be something if he doesn't accept Gatsby's invitation.

Consequence no. 1: if he enters, his life will dramatically and irreversibly change.

Consequence no. 2: if he doesn't enter, his life won't change at all.

A side note: the ripples of World War I haunt this novel, and yet they're not at all explicit. A terrific example of research, both lived and learned, informing the narrative even if specific details about the war aren't in the book. We'll talk more about this when we address setting, or as I think of it, setting as a character in your story.

EXERCISE: Think of your story idea. Answer these three questions:

1. Where are we (place) as it begins?
2. When are we in history, and in the character's life (old, young) as it begins?
3. Who are we (describe the character) as it begins?

Now, create or pick (from your story) an inciting incident arising from those answers. What consequences does it create for your character?

Here's an example:

1. *Where are we as it begins?* A small suburb outside Chicago
2. *When are we in history and in the character's life as it begins?* It's the early 1960s, a turbulent time of racial strife and threats of war. The main character is graduating high school and considering his bright future.
3. *Who are we as it begins?* The main character's father is a lifelong military man, proud of his heritage and hoping his son carries on the family tradition. The main character has other ideas for himself and is in love with a new girl who transferred as the only African American at the high school.

You can see the possibilities here. The coming war in Vietnam, as an example; how might that impact the main character who doesn't want a military future (but perhaps craves his father's approval and doesn't want to be seen as a coward). The father, who wants his son to be brave but is afraid to lose him to an actual war (might the military father be the one to send his son away to avoid the draft? What conflicts does this cause?). The girl the main character loves, who may be the subject of racism. How does the main character react to the idea of fighting at her side? Losing friends? Leaving her to that environment if he joins the military?

Even a simple exercise can spark ideas that just might make into your novel and influence the acts to come.

ACT TWO

After your story's exposition culminates in the inciting incident we discussed above, with all its consequences for your character and the choices presented to them, along comes Act Two. This act forms the bulk of the story to its climax. Act Two is composed of a series of events that both build and complicate the plot. Remember the "pass it" game we played? Think of someone, given them a problem, make it worse, worser, worst? That exercise introduced you to the transition from Act One to Act Two. The "worsening" is also known as rising action. By the middle or so of the story, the character's journey has brought them away from the life they were living, into a new situation that heightens and worsens until a seemingly insurmountable crisis is reached. In our *Jaws* example, the hunt for the shark is on, but the challenges continue to mount well beyond what the characters, thrust as they are in a new and uncertain situation, are capable of dealing with. Quint is obsessed and quite possibly insane. The shark is bigger and more ferocious than they anticipated. The boat, as goes the classic line, really needs to be bigger!

> "Act Two is composed of a series of events that both build and complicate the plot."

In other words, *worse* got *worser* and *worser*. Remember, not every story is an action piece, so the complications that ensnare your character can certainly include rising conflicts that are quiet, subtle, internal, conscience-based, moral, ethical, and the like.

You may hear references to "pinch points" in the second act. These are smaller turning points that occur between the inciting incident in act one and the "worser" event in act two. Pinch points can serve as reminders to the reader of your main character's strengths. They can deliver new information. They can foreshadow what's to come. Think *Star Wars*, when the emperor tells Darth Vader to hunt Luke Skywalker down. It's slightly to the side of the main action in the scene just before it, but it helps keep the narrative pace moving and foreshadows what's to come. It also adds an air of menace to the story.

The first pinch point comes about a quarter of the way through the second act. It occurs after the first plot point we discussed. The character's world has changed because of that first plot point, right? They're still getting their feet under them from that event, and not so successfully in most stories. They're in reaction mode. They haven't figured it all out yet. Whatever they've tried at or to this point, it's not the answer. *Worser*, remember? They're developing a bit of an awareness, though, at the situation they're in. This pinch point marks the period in your story where your character begins to realize things. They acquire information from their failures (and from other characters). Eventually, like around the midpoint of your story, they come to an epiphany. A moment of truth. A decision on which course of action to take. It may not be the right one (we're still in the middle of the story, right?), but it does mark their transition from reaction to action. They embark, they take that action, they think they've got it all figured out, and…

The second pinch point hits! This is roughly three quarters of the way in. It further complicates and frustrates your character's ambitions to change things, fix things, solve things, even understand things. It's that final hill they need to climb. It brings on the third act.

> **EXERCISE:** Take the inciting incident from your first act. How did it impact, affect, or change your character and their situation? Now, take that situation they're in as a result of the incident and make it worse. Why is it worse? What options does your character have to choose from? What choice would they make, based on what you know about them? Why that one? What do you, the writer, think they should do? Is it different from the choice they, the character, would want to make? If so, why?
>
> **KEY:** If it isn't different, why? Is the character, perhaps, a bit too much like you? Something to consider.

ACT THREE

In Act Three, the events you've set in motion lead to a climactic confrontation. A "point of no return," where your main character either succeeds or fails. In *Jaws*, we find Brody alone on a sinking boat, clinging perilously to the mast as the shark barrels toward him. Resolution of this conflict—shark explodes, survivors swim home—brings about de-escalation as the events of the story wind down and the characters return to the world they were thrown from in Act One.

Of course, they won't be the same, having gone through the events of the story. As we turn the last page, we find ourselves wondering how life will be for them now.

> **EXERCISE:** Fix the issue you created for your character.

The Timeline

How stories go from beginning to end can vary widely. Sometimes, the "beginning" isn't in the character's present. Or it is, but the next scene isn't chronological; the storyline moves to the past or to someone else's view of the same moment. Story timelines can absolutely be played with and manipulated, always in service of the goal: tell the story in a compelling way.

Let's look at some of these timeline structures. One of them may take your story to the next level.

> "In Act Three, the events you've set in motion lead to a climactic confrontation."

Chronological

Linear or chronological storytelling may be the easiest way to approach your story when you're starting out. Begin at the beginning and lay out the events in the order they'll happen (or at least the order you think they may happen) all the way to the end. As you'll see in the revision section, when you have everything laid out that way, or when you have a draft completed, you may feel that a different order is called for. Perhaps there's a moment in the chronology where you say, "More than a quick flashback is needed here to explain why this matters." You may then decide to take the story back to the past for a chapter. All good! That's what the revision process is there for. Right now, it's all about getting your thoughts down without too much regard for whether they work.

> **EXERCISE:** In a few sentences, write your story idea chronologically. How it begins, what happens next, and how it ends. If you don't know, that's ok! Make it up. Something might stick with you.

Nonlinear

Nonlinear story structure can be fractured and out of chronological order. It can switch time periods and characters from whose standpoints the story is told. David Mitchell's magnificent *Cloud Atlas* and Vonnegut's *Slaughterhouse Five* are well-known examples of this, but think of any story you've read or seen where the present action arrives at a moment in which the character is looking at an old photo, or sees someone that stops them in their tracks. The very next scene is in the past, and they're a younger version of themselves, and by the time we're back in the present, we understand the gravity and meaning of that moment. That's nonlinear storytelling.

> **EXERCISE:** Take what you wrote chronologically and start it in the middle (the second or third sentence you wrote when thinking about "what happens next). Think of, or make up, a moment that happens there (a character sees something, hears a song, runs into someone we don't yet know is an old love). Make that the first sentence. Now, go back to the beginning and make that "what happens next." Where does that take you? Does anything change from the chronological sentences you did? Why?

Circular

In this type of structure, the story ends where it began. The characters undergo changes such that when the end comes and we're back where it all started, we have a new perspective. If you're familiar with the James Cameron film *Titanic*, you know that as the story begins we meet an old woman named Rose at the beginning, aboard a modern research vessel searching for the sunken ocean liner. By the end, we're back to the same modern boat in the same time period and location as the beginning, but we have an entirely new perspective on Rose and her presence atop the water, in the spot where the Titanic, and her great love, went down.

> **EXERCISE:** Start your story sentences with the end, then go to the beginning. End at the end, again. As you do this, what's coming to you in terms of ideas about things to reference, that might not make sense at first but will take on resonance later (the ship's rail, the necklace)? What do we, the readers, know that we didn't the first time we saw the end of the story?

Parallel

What's this one? Two books sewn together? Not quite. Parallel storylines are multiple plotlines, each following its respective track and ultimately tying together through an event that affects all the characters and bumps them on their journeys. The classic example? Fitzgerald's *Great Gatsby* (which, if you haven't guessed yet, is an absolute masterclass in writing a novel). Think of it: Jay Gatsby bought a magnificent home across the water from his one great, lost love Daisy. Daisy's husband Tom is cheating on her with the wild wife of a gas station owner. Nick, the observer, from whose point of view these parallel stories are told, is pulled into each arc, bearing willing and unwilling witness to the events until a road accident simultaneously binds the stories together and throws them to their outcomes.

> **EXERCISE:** Take your chronological storyline. Now, create a similarly chronological plotline for a different character. It may be someone in the story already, or someone you make up right now for this exercise. How do those two plotlines overlap? What do they have in common with each other? Maybe they're in love with the same person, live in the same city, have the same job...

Chapter Four

THE POINT OF VIEW GUIDE

THIS IS A GOOD TIME TO START THINKING ABOUT THE NARRATIVE POINT OF VIEW, or "POV." Who's telling us the story? When we read, will "I" or "me" or "we" tell it? Or will "she," "her," "he," "they" tell it?

First person ("I") may offer the clearest path to a story told in a linear fashion. You can still use flashbacks and internal monologues (which we'll touch upon) to enhance the characters and story. Third person allows the writer greater flexibility and a degree of omniscience when it comes to the cast of characters.

Is the concept of POV still a bit murky? Are you uncertain which point of view is the best one for your story?

Think of it like a dinner table.

Imagine the story you want to write takes place in a dining room, and the characters you want to portray are seated around a large table. From whose perspective would you like to tell the story?

Here are your choices:

If you want the story's narrator to be "I," (as in, "I woke up with a bad headache and a worse feeling…"), go ahead and take a seat at the table. With this POV, the story will flow from the character's first person-eye view, speaking externally to the others and internally to us about what they see. If you want that "I" to know what everyone is thinking, you have a decision, and the choices each carry consequences of their own. For example, if the "I" of your first-person story knows what one person thinks of the person next to her, maybe it's because the "I" knows that person so intimately that reading them is second nature. If that's the case, *why* (our old friend)? What is the nature of their relationship? Could they be wrong in their read of the situation, and what consequences to the characters and story might flow from that error?

As you can already see, if you're telling the story from a first person "I" perspective, the rules of your story dictate how "I" knows things about people other than herself. The nature of the relationship she has with others may explain and establish how she knows things. Perhaps the accuracy of what she knows, or thinks she knows, is one of the conflicts in the story. She calculates how someone will react and gets it spectacularly wrong. Maybe she's psychic and absolutely knows what everyone's thinking. What might that do to her?

First person point of view offers a certain intimacy to the reader. It's like speaking to a friend or confidant, and it can also enhance the "attitude" of the story by adopting a tone suitable to the narrative. Hopeful, snarky, angry, defeated, triumphant—a lot can be communicated by the voice, whether the narrator is the centerpiece or an observer off to one side.

Let's go back to the dinner table and try a different perspective. Your narrator (they may not literally narrate; this is a reference to the character from whose perspective the story flows to us) is no longer at the table. They're in the doorway, with a clear view of everyone in the room. They can see what each person is doing, who they're speaking to, who's getting the bulk of their attention, who they're stealing glances at. Maybe they can hear a bit of conversation, but they don't know what anyone's thinking. This is a pure third person perspective. We the readers hear about a swath of characters and events, and those won't be limited to what one person sees, or was present to witness, in the way first person can result in.

Perhaps the observer of the dinner table can hear all the conversations, internal and external, and can illuminate what we the readers understand by showing us the backstories, memories, and experiences of some or all of the dinner guests. That's third person omniscient. Like the camera in a film, this point of view can switch between characters, between plot lines, move in close for an intimate, even claustrophobic view, or widen out and allow the reader to see the world in total. Third person point of view offers something the others can't always do: contrast. The action (internal and external) taking place among the characters and between plot arcs can be seen side by side. When used in a decisive manner, this can be a powerful tool for illustrating the contradictions, difficult choices and divergent paths people thrust into the same circumstance can take.

Perhaps the third person narrator isn't in the doorway, but instead has stepped into the room and is standing behind one person. They see things mainly from that person's perspective, and while they may have insight into that person's thoughts, they don't have any insight with the others. This is a more limited form of third person. The story is filtered through and influenced by one person's perspective more than the others.

There is another, albeit trickier, point of view available. Second person narrative point of view, in which the narrative voice references "you" ("You have entered...the Twilight Zone") is a daring choice for an entire novel. It may serve a short story better, as the overarching challenge of this POV is the difficulty of making the reader feel that they're a part of the story, as they must for this POV to be effective.

Take the opening line from the wonderful novel by Andrew Sean Greer, *The Confessions of Max Tivoli*:

"We are each the love of someone's life."

Let's shift the POV to first person singular. *I am the love of someone's life*. See how the meaning changes? The possible events that unspool from an observation like "We are each the love of someone's life" are different from those that are suggested by "I am the love of someone's life." You can feel the openness of your writing choices present in the first, plural version narrow a bit with a simple shift to singular. It feels like the statement is directed at someone specific.

Now, shift that line to second person POV:

"You are the love of someone's life."

See what just happened? You, as the reader, aren't stepping into a story of a man who ages out of time with the rest of the world. Instead, the reader (standing in the shoes of that mysterious "you") is trying to figure out who, what and where the love of "your" life might be. It can shift the entire tone of the book from meditative to thriller. That may be a decision the author makes, to bring the readers into the story, and in short sections it may be a powerful jolt, but unless there's a strong and well-defined purpose, this can also prevent the reader from truly experiencing the story as it plays out.

Some second-person narrative devices make infrequent use of the word "you," offering instead an indirect approach. Take a simple sentence: "The clouds moved fast." If we change it a bit, to "Those clouds are moving fast," it sounds like it's addressing us. Again, that's a tool that can be used, like any other, but it's important to have a clear intention around second person.

I had an interesting and illuminating experience with POV while writing my second novel. The first draft was in first person. I was quite close to the main character, and it felt like the right way to tell the story. When I finished, I set the draft aside to gain some objectivity and perspective, then returned to it to consider revisions.

Something was deeply wrong with it. The narrative felt dominated by interior monologues, and the cast of characters were too vague. But I wasn't quite sure how to remedy the problem.

Then, as an experiment, I took a few sections of the novel and moved them into third person.

Here's a short paragraph from that second novel, *The Night Language*, in first person:

"We remained in the portrait room together, deep into the night. As exhausted and worried as he was, Philip couldn't close his eyes. He couldn't miss so simple a thing as two people who'd lost, alone and silent, speaking in a night language only they understood."

> "Don't be afraid to make a different choice from the one we start with. Those unexpected changes are often the source of the real stuff that raises your piece from *meh* to good to published."

The main character from whose vantage point the story is told, in both present and flashback, is Alamayou (there's a larger issue that the first-or-third question really threw into stark relief, of a secret identity, that I won't get into— I guess you'll just have to read it!). He presents us a moment of observation regarding a character close to him, Philip. When told in first person, can you see how questions arise? How does the main character, Alamayou, know what Philip is afraid of missing? How does Alamayou know any of what's going on in Philip's thoughts?

Now, the same passage moved to third person:

"They remained in the portrait room together, deep into the night. As exhausted and worried as he was, Philip couldn't close his eyes. He couldn't miss so simple a thing as two people who'd lost, alone and silent, speaking in a night language only they understood."

We're in an omniscient POV now, and the issues noted above are no longer present. What's more, we the reader can observe Alamayou (with Queen Victoria in the scene), and we can take a moment from the outer action (two people in a room together), observed by another character, and from it we learn not only what's happening in this moment, but we learn as well what's in Philip's head and heart.

I quickly realized that the entire story needed to be in third person. I also realized that it was a far greater task than merely changing pronouns from "I" to "he." For example, in the passage above from the novel, notice the verb tense. It's past. If it remained in first person and was in past tense, a question immediately arises: is the character telling us this story as a recollection? If so, where is he now?

It also has the effect of draining the story of its dramatic tension. When life-endangering moments come, we already know he's fine, or else he couldn't be telling the story in retrospect (unless he's a ghost, and that rule has already been established in the novel). The stakes just lowered.

Ok, so what if it's first-person, present tense?

"We remain in the portrait room together…"

Aside from the perspective issue noted above (how does "I" know what Philip is thinking?), the author has a decision to make: how much of the novel will be told in interior monologues, in real time, and how interesting is that for the reader to spend time with? "I think about…". "I walk into the room…". "I realize that I'll never…".

In my case, the answer was pretty obvious. For a different, meditative sort of book, or a story where the main character's fragile, unreliable state of mind is the central tenet, first person might be a great fit. For *The Night Language*, it wasn't. Revision time!

The moral? POV, like so many components of our stories, is a choice we make. The reasons underlying those choices may change as we write, and again as we revise. We shouldn't be afraid to make a different choice from the one we start with. Those unexpected changes are often the source of the real stuff that raises your piece from *meh* to good to published.

> **EXERCISE:** Take one of the small pieces of your idea from the plot arc section. It can be chronological, parallel, or one of the others. Now, step into that dining room with it. If you have someone you can do this exercise with, tell the story out loud. If not, write it down. Try telling them/writing down the story in first person ("That morning, I woke up with a strange feeling…").
>
> Next, tell it/write it in second person ("That morning, you woke up with a strange feeling…"). Now, do it in third person ("That morning, she woke up with a strange feeling…").

What do these various POV changes do to the possibilities your story contains? What does it do to the tension, credibility, engagement factors? Do these different approaches generate different ideas on what might happen next? Write those down!

Chapter Five

THE CHARACTER IDENTIFIERS

BEFORE WE BEGIN, YOU MIGHT THINK THIS SECTION LOOKS LIKE A WHOLE LOT OF EXERCISES, but don't worry! Getting to know your characters is one of the joys of writing. Think of this as a party. The party is your story idea, as well as the events in that story's inner and outer world. You're asking questions to get to know the people populating that party. As your characters answer these questions, you consider how those answers might fit, influence, and change your story. And of course, *why* they do that. *Why* do they answer the questions that way? What is it about them, their lives, their situation, upbringing, and experiences, that make them answer that way? Why does their answer impact the story?

> "What happens in the world you create affects your character's journey, and what your character goes through will affect the world they inhabit."

Welcome to the party—let's dive in!

The arc of your character moves in time, or in counterpoint, to the arc of your story. What happens in the world you create affects your character's journey, and what your character goes through will affect the world they inhabit.

OUTER WORLD EVENTS
War comes and times get tough. Divorce splits a family apart. Infidelity crumbles trust between partners and their respective friend circles. The rebellious child comes home and disrupts a family's careful order. The job offer comes, but it's far from everything and fear sets in as to how life will change for one never away from home before.

INNER WORLD EVENTS

Your character finally, fearfully comes out to her/his family. They fall in or out (or both) of first or late-in-life love. They struggle with a secret addiction, crippling self-doubt, undiagnosed disorders, and no one sees. No one hears or understands how badly they need help, and so they turn to precisely the wrong people.

These outer and inner events can both be present; in most stories they are. Take this scenario: An elderly man must make the difficult choice to put his longtime spouse into an assisted living facility because she's struggling with Alzheimer's. He sees her every day, and in that way maintains the connection even as her memory begins to fade. Then the pandemic hits, and he can't visit her in person for a year. What does he find when at last he's able to see her? What does she remember of him or their life together? Does the act of seeing her put him in danger health-wise? Does the vaccine exist yet?

The characters' inner and outer worlds, each with their respective conflicts, collide against and run alongside each other.

It's not just what your characters do when up against the events of the story that will shape their arcs. *How* and *why* your characters do what they do when up against conflict reveals a lot about them. Remember the yellow light exercise? As they come to the intersection—the event that changes as they approach—they have decisions to make. What they do, and how they handle whatever happens next, reveals things about them.

If I may once again draw from one of my books by way of illustration:

As I mentioned, *The Luminist* was based very loosely on the life of an early photographic pioneer, Julia Margaret Cameron. My research took me deep into a biography of her. Over the course of 400+ pages, I found one line that stuck with me over the next several weeks (hello, flypaper effect!). Just a simple sentence in that biography, informing the reader that she'd lost a child at birth. Not an uncommon event at that time, sadly. But that single small piece of her, set against the research I'd done on Ceylon and early photographic works came together to create an indelible image of a woman who lost a child at a time when the only way to hold a memory was memory itself. Memories fade over time; they distend and grow faint. She lost her child and feared the day she might no longer be able to clearly recollect her baby's face. As a result, she dived headlong into the emerging art and science of photography, obsessed with the need to "hold beauty still" so it's never lost again.

When you consider your main character and the secondary characters, you may find it not all different from your research into the larger story: it may not be the "big picture" of the character as a detective or a scientist or fallen priest. Rather, it's something small that your emerging story is circling around. A single moment you can't get out of your head. One event that you want to plant in someone's life to see what happens. One fact about them, like the loss of a child at birth, set against the larger world of your story. One thing they said, or did, or that you know of them. You plant that one thing into your story, and see what it does. See how it changed who that person was the moment before that thing, and ask of them (and yourself as the writer), what would happen. Why would it happen?

A person, in the end, is the sum of all that's happened to them.

The way a character changes over the course of your story because of actions and experiences—theirs, others', the world's—coupled with their reflection on those events, their decisions because of them, and their own actions in response to them, forms not only the story's arc over the course of its various acts, but the characters' arcs as well.

> **EXERCISE:** Using your story as it's developed (particularly through our research, timeline, and POV sections), choose two events. One should be an outer event such as war, a political issue, something in the background that is a part of the social fabric of the world your character inhabits, like racism, inequality, poverty, etc.). One should be inner (a divorce, a birth, a death, a geographic or emotional move, etc.). How does each affect your character? How do they influence/affect/intertwine with each other? What does your character do because of them, and why?

Now, let's start a conversation. This is a great exercise to do with a partner, but it's also really helpful to ask and answer these questions by yourself, thinking of the character and what they would say. Begin with your main character:

What's their name? Is this the name they were born with? Did they ever want to change it? If so (like you don't know what question is coming), why?

Where were they born? When is their birthday? How do they feel about their age at the moment we meet them("I wish I was old enough to..."; "I don't feel this old...")? Why?

Does their age change over the course of the story? By how much?

Who is the most influential person in their life? Is it a family member? A friend? A celebrity or athlete? Is it a good or bad influence? Why?

What do they look like? How do others see them? Handsome, beautiful, repellant, scary, laughable, clumsy, graceful? Why? Does this jibe with how they see themselves? Why or why not?

What's their personality like? Funny, clever, boring, irritable, quiet, shy, brave, awkward? Why?

What's their best and worst trait? How does that trait play into the story? Why?

Where do they live? Where do they *wish* they lived? Why?

How do they live in relation to the immediate world around them, and why? For example, your character lives in NY, but they're juggling two minimum wage gigs and trying, not always successfully, to make rent. That may not be a critical part of the story, but it certainly will influence how they interact with their immediate surroundings, not to mention other people.

Who do they live with? Is this the person they want to live with, or is there someone else, real or imagined? Why?

What's their favorite food? What's their go-to staple? Do they cook, or does someone else do it? Why? As you play with this, think about their relation to the world. This will help you keep their eating habits in line with their economic and social attributes. For example, if they're living just above the poverty line, their diet is likely different than someone who's well off. This may also factor into their physical appearance. Can they afford a gym? Are they shredded because of manual labor? Are they softening because of a poor diet? Are they living in the middle of a war zone, and they're experiencing rationing and shortages? Do they live off the land? Is it their land?

What do they wear most often? How often do they "dress up" and how do they feel about doing so? What can they afford? How does what they wear communicate their inner lives, as far as they're concerned? Do they overly sexualize themselves to make up for a lack of confidence in their appearance? Do they dress way down to disappear among people? Do they wear baggy clothes because they're obsessed with their weight? Do they wear punk regalia to broadcast their rebelliousness? And is what they think they're conveying what others actually see? Why?

You can see how each seemingly simple question leads to multiple avenues.

That's a lot of opportunity for you to play with the shape of your characters. You may also see how this information plays out in your story. Some or all of it may not even make it in, but the character is taking a more intimate, familiar shape in your head. When you write about them in a particular circumstance, you've given yourself guidance on how they might act and how they might feel.

Now, do this for your other characters. Try to answer these questions differently than you did with the main character. This will create nice contradictions and contrasts that you can put to work in the story.

As you think of your characters, don't be afraid to draw upon yourself for inspiration, especially to get you started. Giving them an interest or a passion of yours will help make them more vivid to you. Don't worry that you're just writing about yourself. Those pieces of you may well drop out of the story as you progress, and the characters start asserting their own agency, but it may offer you a door into them to start you off. It may also ease your first attempts at writing their internal lives. That can be a bit daunting, sketching out the inner world of someone you're only just getting to know. Use yourself as a reference—how would you feel, and (of course) why? Then ask yourself, based upon what you know of the character, do they feel the same? Why or why not? And with that, your character is on her/his way to forming.

Chapter Six

THE CHARACTER DEVELOPMENT FORMULA

YOUR CHARACTERS' TRAITS, THEIR ACTIONS AND REACTIONS, THEIR ENTANGLEMENTS AND FRICTIONS WITH EACH OTHER, will all influence the plot points of your story. As with your character's traits, if it helps to ease your way into the story, think of your own relationships. Think of others in your life, and how you'd define the dominant theme of each person as they relate to you. Love, lust, enemy, friend, frenemy, casual, intrigued, "it's complicated." Our own lives can serve as jumping off points to conceiving characters. Again, they'll eventually assert their own characteristics as you write your way into them and the story around them.

Here are some general thoughts to keep in mind as you write your way into your characters:

Subtext rules!

Most people aren't explicit about their feelings, motives, secrets or wants. What we observe of them—their outward behavior—is based on an interior life we can't know. Moreover, that interior life is difficult for even the most articulate of us to grasp, let alone communicate. Do you find yourself thinking of how you feel moment to moment, and then tracing that feeling back in an exacting, insightful, and fully informed way to the formative experience that generated it, then threading it back through to your present, taking precise note along the way of how that old experience now influences you?

Yeah, neither do I. And neither should your characters, at least not to excess. In your writing—really, in the revision process—you should strive for balance between the interior and exterior life and actions of your characters. Too many monologues can really slow the pace of your story. People reveal their thoughts and feelings in small actions, in "tells." The nervous habit, the thousand-mile stare, the posture of the body. Ever have the experience of a difficult conversation made all the more so by the closed-off posture of the person you're speaking to? The folded arms, the way their body tilts back as if they're trying to escape the room altogether? Those "tells," the physical gestures, told you what they felt about the situation, and perhaps about you. Subtext!

Of course, there will be times when you'll need to reveal a character's thoughts (in keeping with the POV, of course). The outer scene may seem to be relatively normal—say, a crowded city street where an officer is directing traffic—but your character is terrified of the police. Contrasting the routine outer world with the torment of the character's inner life at that moment can serve the story in a number of ways: mood, conflict revelation, clarifying and demonstrating motivation. These moments, when used in proportion to passages that serve to drive the story forward, help the reader understand and empathize with the characters' primary reasons for doing what they do. They're starving, they're protecting their children, they're lonely, they're consumed by jealousy, they're over the moon with excitement, they're in love.

Try this: Write out a scene from your story, or a moment from your life, where there's more going on than meets the eye. You run into an old friend with whom there's tension that was never resolved. You're reassuring your child, but you're actually more uncertain or nervous than you let on. You interview for a job, and you project confidence, but secretly you worry that you're not what they're looking for. Now, write the scene again, but this time leave out your internal thoughts. Write only about what the reader sees or hears. The dialogue, the gestures, the world around the characters. Write this to completion. Once that's done, write how you or your character was really feeling in the margins, wherever such feelings arose.

Walk away from it for a bit, then come back. As you read the story, ask yourself: can I tell from the gestures or from the way the dialogue flows what's really going on? If I saw this character just before this scene, would that give me the context to understand how she really feels here? If the answer is yes, you've captured the subtext of the scene. If the answer is no, and the moments before this scene wouldn't reveal anything, then it may be a place to drop in some interior dialogue to better reveal the truth of the character in that scene, at that moment.

Here are some other exercises you can incorporate to help draw the contours of your characters:

1. If you consider your character largely good, give them a flaw or two.
2. If you consider them largely bad, give them a certain morality. A code

they live by, that consistently guides them. Think of the killer or killers in literature and film (the books and show featuring the serial killer Dexter come to mind). Just as the protagonist is guided by a certain set of rules, so too can the antagonist be similarly guided, and it happens that their rules make the life of the protagonist miserable until the climax.

3. Give them some major life events (some, all, or none of these may be germane to your story and therefore make their way in. But knowing this about the characters, in just the same way that knowing a friend's father has passed, helps place their perspectives, emotional reactions, and life choices into context). Some examples of these include:

    Trauma (assault at an earlier point in time; a dire diagnosis and the fallout from that; physical or emotional abuse)

    Thresholds crossed (lost virginity; passing of a parent; first vote or drink; first time driving)

    Childhood experiences

4. Give them things that they ruminate on regularly. Perhaps they long for travel. Perhaps they're trans and are only just beginning to imagine another, different life. Maybe they're frustrated musicians who long to shred onstage with Iron Maiden. What do they fantasize about in those moments when, to the outside world, they seem quite far away?

5. Give them friends at different points in their lives, whether those people make it into the story or not. Who was their best friend in kindergarten? Who was their first crush? Who did they confide in during high school? Why them?

6. Give them some hobbies. What do they do to relax? To find inspiration? What is that thing they always turn to in times of stress, or when they want to make sense of the world around them?

7. Take an incident from their past (again, not necessarily one that will be included in the story) and write about its impact on the character's present. An example might include a childhood accident that left a scar they're deeply self-conscious about, or a limp that they worked hard to overcome, or loss of certain memories they're trying to recover.

8. Take a personality trait and write a description of it through action. Don't name it or define it. Write it out as one who knows them might observe it as it manifests. An example of this could include a high state of anxiety

that manifests in the form of the character relentlessly picking at their own skin.

9. Describe their favorite personal space. Do they find peace in a well-stocked, lushly appointed kitchen? Do they retreat to their bedroom when they need some breathing room?
10. Write a short piece about your characters at a different time and place in their lives, making use of what you know about them, and with an eye toward discovering some things you don't know.
11. Take a scene from your story (even one you haven't written yet—perhaps one you've thought about, or that you keep seeing in your head) and write it in first person, from your character's point of view. In other words, step into your character's shoes. Become them, and in first person, tell the story of that scene or moment.
12. Think about a key struggle in your story. A crisis, a turning point, an event which places your character in a difficult situation. What skill might they need to deal with it? Do they already have it? If so, write about what they would do to acquire it, if they didn't already have it. In the classic film *The Karate Kid*, Daniel is helpless until Mr. Miyagi helps him acquire the necessary skills to overcome his primary conflict. Remember, one of your character's best teachers is failure. Everyone loves to read about overcoming adversity!
13. Now, return to the yellow light game. Having created some additional material around your characters, has the decision they made the first time at that intersection changed? Why?

For all of these, once you've imagined answers, ask yourself (say it with me!) *why?*

What are we doing with exercises like these?

You may recall me saying that I knew I was ready to start writing a piece when it felt less like something I'd made up and more like a memory of something that happened to me. The process of researching, structuring, living with and within the story as it takes shape, is how I come to know the story from the inside. I know how it is to live in it, the way we all know how it was to live in the home we grew up in. Home stays with us because it *is* us. Who we became can be found in the walls. Who we wanted to be could be glimpsed through the windows. Our memories live there because that's where we did the things that we carried forward, into the next phase of our lives and the next.

When you write your way into your story, or as here, your characters, you're creating that level of intimacy whether you realize it or not. Because of that intimacy, you develop an innate, instinctive sense of what the right choice is on any given issue in your story.

Think of your closest friend. Now, think of a situation you and they/them might find yourselves in together. Imagine them making a choice they would never make, or acting in a way that's way out of character for them. See how weird that feels, to think of them doing that? Can you hear the dissonance in your mind when you consider the possibility of them acting that way?

Ask yourself, how can you be so sure of them?

The answer's pretty simple, right? You know them. You truly know them. So how do you get to know your characters this well? How do you get to that place where you can answer the "yellow-light test" for each of them with no hesitation, because that's how intimately you understand them?

The answer is the same as it is with your best friend. Your knowledge of them didn't come from answering a series of questions when you first met. It came from life. You spent time with them, and over that time, you learned, and you liked what you learned, so you kept going.

Think of these exercises as the host of a party you're attending. You've approached the host to inquire about a particular guest who you find interesting but have never seen before. You ask some basic questions about them, to introduce them to your mind. But to get to know them? You have to meet them where they are, across the room or on the terrace, and engage with them. Talk to them. Listen to them. Spend time with them. Every conversation between people who don't know each other starts with questions ("What's your name?" "How do you know the host?" "Are you falling for me like I'm falling for you?"– ok, maybe not that one). But soon, the questions cease, and conversations begin. Listening and learning begin.

The next time you see this person whom you just might become friends or more with, you don't sit them down and outline the next two years of your not-yet-existing relationship down to the day. You don't point them to that outline and tell them "Ok, no matter what we've learned about each other, no matter what's happened between now and then, no matter how we've changed and surprised each other and moved in ways we didn't expect, on that day X months or years from now, you HAVE to do exactly as I've written right here."

You don't do any of those things. You just spend time, and over time, you become close enough to know what they'd do in a given situation.

That's how it goes in life. In writing life, you write your way there.

The material we're creating together is invaluable for getting you started, and for instilling the confidence to commence your journey into the story. It can be a bit intimidating to just jump in with no sense of any direction, people, or destination (it can also be exhilarating!). But it all allows you time with your story and characters, and over that time you'll come to know them better. But—and I know I've said it before—as you get to truly, deeply know them, they'll start making their own choices. Never be afraid to let them! Don't be afraid to let your story and characters wander off the outline. Never be afraid to go down a blind alley and get a bit lost. Or a lot lost. You may discard the whole adventure, but you'll have spent that time with the people of your story. You'll have learned more about them, and that will inform the piece in so many ways. Lean into it and see what happens.

We've seen the way your story arcs through its various acts toward the climax and the end. But how do the characters in that story arc? Here's how:

They change alongside their changing circumstances, though not necessarily in the same direction.

Don't worry—you don't necessarily need to know *how* they change before you start (you may have a general, 30,000-foot level thought as to where they start out physically, emotionally, spiritually, economically, socially, etc., and you may have an equally vague thought as to whether they remain that way at the end). All you really need to know is what happens in the story. As we've touched on, and will see more of in the outline phase, this knowledge of "what happens" is acquired, and certainly it morphs into unexpected directions as you write your way into the story.

Though you may not be familiar with the labels, you know character arcs well! Think of Harry Potter. His arc is transformational. He figuratively and literally undergoes a dramatic, heroic change from a shy and uncertain boy to a courageous, magic-infused warrior. The so-called "hero's journey" is common in any form of story-telling you can think of. But that certainly doesn't mean it's played out. When done with heart, it's a truly satisfying arc for readers to follow.

A different, though in some ways related, arc is often referred to as a positive arc. I like Ebenezer Scrooge as an example of this. The character starts out quite negatively, and through a series of escalating conflicts and events, they manage to reach a new understanding of his place in the world. In doing so, he effects a great deal of change on the world around him. The arc of the character and the arc of the story move in time.

A negative character arc sees the character on a path to darkness, or at least to great difficulties that will test their resilience, and perhaps their soul. Michael Corleone in *The Godfather* is an excellent example of this; his early pronouncement that he is in no way like his father or family is sorely tested in a series of escalating external and internal conflicts, until that marvelous moment at the end of the first film when Michael, assuring his wife Kay that he's clear of the mafia fray his family was embroiled in, closes the door in her face as his supplicants prepare to kiss his ring. The downfall, the loss of self, the journey away from the promise of the character's early life, is the point of this arc, and it can offer us a mirror in which we can see our own striving and the price we pay.

Though it seems odd, there actually is such a thing as a static character arc. The character remains the same throughout the events of the story, despite all that's dynamically set in motion around them. Action plots often feature such a character; James Bond comes to mind, as do Sherlock Holmes, Miss Marple, Hercule Poirot, and so on (see a pattern?). They're unflappable, often stoic, seemingly unbeatable, and all too often, dull to read, dependent as they are on the pyrotechnics of the plot to involve the reader. They also are in many cases series characters, and they rely on the audience's knowledge of them from past iterations, thereby foregoing the need for any history, backstory, or context. Use this sort of arc, if that's where you're leaning, in a fully informed way. There's a wonderful old screenwriting adage: you can have the world's most incredible car chase, but if you don't care about the characters in the car, it's just a lot of noise.

Whichever arc your story resembles (and it may incorporate a few), the reader needs to be emotionally invested in your characters. That means your characters need to be emotionally invested in the story unfolding around them. They need to engage with the world, and with each other.

The way your characters engage with each other should mirror real life, no matter how "out there" your story might be. Some people in our lives are complimentary. Their skillsets fill gaps in our own, technically, emotionally, socially. We've all experienced moments where we can't quite bring ourselves to do something, and a trusted friend or relative nudges us the rest of the way there.

Think of the character of Q in the James Bond stories. 007 may be physically adept and cunning, but without Q's technological wizardry, most of those stories would end with a dead secret agent.

On the emotional front, perhaps your character can't bring herself to communicate with her mother or an ex. But some communication needs to take place in that section of the story dealing with a custody issue, an old wound come roaring back to life, a family secret that's finally and devastatingly revealed. A supporting character can act in counterpoint to the main character's dilemma. They may be the mediator of the family, or merely someone with no emotional stake in that particular person or situation, so they don't care about speaking their mind. In these examples, the skillsets of surrounding characters support and supplant the main character's shortcomings.

Your character's engagement with others in the arc of the story can also be oppositional. The love interest who's *not* interested. The challenger to the main character's throne (whatever that may be) who takes it, requiring renewed dedication and commitment from the main character. The foil who's always, seemingly, one step ahead of our main character.

You may see a bit of a theme here—one way stories pique our interest in a character is not only placing them at the heart of a key conflict, but identifying them as a cause of that conflict, whether internal or external.

Speaking of which . . .

Chapter Seven

THE STORY MOMENTUM GENERATOR

CONFLICT IS THE STRUGGLE BETWEEN OPPOSING FORCES. Circumstances pull the characters in directions they don't want to go, or never dreamt of going, or can't go for fear of never returning. Tensions rise.

Classically, conflict is thought of as embodying two overarching types—Internal and External—and falling into one or more of these buckets:

Character vs. self
Character vs. character
Character vs. nature
Character vs. supernatural
Character vs. technology
Character vs. society

Internal conflicts involve the characters' struggles with their own beliefs, wants, needs, weaknesses or impulses; in other words, the forces that shaped their lives. This conflict plays out inside their minds, but manifests externally. The classic tale of Dr. Jekyll's struggle to control the feral, ferocious impulses of his internal desires made physical in the form of Dr. Hyde provides a wonderful illustration of the internal conflict playing out against the outside world.

External conflicts play out as struggles between the character and an outside force. Something, or someone, outside themselves and beyond their control, stands in their way. How the character navigates that struggle forms a strong component of the story.

Whether internal or external, the stronger the force(s) arrayed against your character, the sharper and more relatable that character will be.

Life, as you might be thinking, almost always throws both such conflict types at us.

Your characters are what drive the story and its various elements. It's through them that we experience what happens, regardless of POV. The way they change—as well as the way they experience, think about, and act upon those changes—dynamically moves the story through its arcs to the conclusion. The lessons they learn, and the ways those lessons move them from who they were to who they become, tie us emotionally into the story.

Here are some ideas for investing your story with conflict.

WHAT KIND OF CONFLICT BEST FITS YOUR STORY?

Think about the type of story you've shaped to this point. What is it? A dramatic telling of unearthed family secrets? A love story set against a looming catastrophe? A closely observed character portrait of a writer's struggles juxtaposed against a newly discovered journal from a long dead writer?

The sort of story you're planning will dictate the types of conflicts that story will most benefit from. Character vs. character? Character vs. supernatural force? Don't forget that as your characters go up against these obstacles, they'll experience emotions concerning their struggle. That's prime territory for exploring character vs. self.

> "Whatever type of conflict your story contains, the reader should understand and be convinced of the reason why it matters so much that your character faces and overcomes that conflict."

WHY DOES IT MATTER?

Whatever type of conflict your story contains, the reader should understand and be convinced of the reason why it matters so much that your character faces and overcomes that conflict. That means the conflict needs to make sense within the rules of the story. The skills, reactions, experiences, and resources your character acquires in order to resolve the conflict shouldn't take the reader by surprise or violate the rules you've set up. In other words, avoid the *deus ex machina* (i.e., don't drop stuff in out of nowhere). If your character has some extraordinary ability that will come into play, the story should introduce that and pace its development from a trait your character possesses (whether they realize it or not) to a conflict of its own they must grapple with, to the means of overcoming their adversary (whether a person, place, situation, feeling, etc.).

THREATEN YOUR CHARACTER

Who do they love the most? What's the one thing they must have, or else? *Threaten it.* Threaten it in the confines of the story. It could be an idea, person, career. Whatever that holy grail is for your character, put it in harm's way. Drop an obstacle between the character and their goal. The conflict arises when that thing your character must have is threatened and they can't get to it. Is it the great love of their life? Drop in a rival for their love. Or a war that comes between them, stranding them on either side of the seemingly impenetrable skirmish line. Send them away from each other and make it really hard to come back. You get the idea.

FORCE THE MAIN CHARACTER AND THE CONFLICT TOGETHER

Put your character and the struggle they're going to have to deal with on a collision course. If your main character never reconciled with her father over an unforgivable transgression, their paths should cross and your plot should squeeze down her choices as she moves through the story, until it's clear that there's no other way but for her to find her father where he is and face what happened.

MAKE THEIR CHOICES REALLY HARD!

If you're familiar with William Styron's deeply moving novel (or perhaps the film version with Meryl Streep) *Sophie's Choice*, you know that it's but one example of the way literature is full of nearly impossible decisions. They wrench our emotions and make us dread the moment of truth, when the character finally decides and faces the consequences of that action. But they also keep us turning pages, no? Make it as difficult as possible for your character to contend with the conflict, and don't forget: the character will have feelings about the choices they face. There's your character vs. self conflict.

On a related note:

DON'T PROTECT YOUR CHARACTERS FROM THE PLOT . . . OR FROM YOU

Let your characters fail. I know, it's hard. Harder than you realize. If you're a parent, or observed your own parent(s) struggle with their feelings as you moved inexorably toward a heartbreak everyone but you saw coming, you get this feeling. Someone you care about is going to get hurt. Perhaps, really badly hurt. Maybe even killed. Every fiber of your being wants to head it off or take the blow for them…or at least let them avoid the worst of it. Don't.

For your kids, it's a learning experience they need to go through. For your character, it's a plot point your story needs. Characters need conflicts to successfully overcome, and they can't be easy or else readers don't care the way you want them to. So yes, you may care deeply for your characters. They may represent you, or people you love. Acknowledge that, then show their fears. Show their flaws. Let them stumble into difficult things without a net. Let them get good and lost, break things, lose people, and lose hope. You may find that you don't need to rescue them. They'll tell you how they intend to rescue themselves.

Based on what we've covered so far, you're probably already seeing the possibilities that conflict brings to the arcs of your story. It bumps against your characters and sends them careening in directions that they, in the context of their written lives, didn't expect. Perhaps it will send your characters in directions *you* didn't expect when you completed your outline. Not only is that ok, it's wonderful and something to hope for. We'll talk more about that in our discussion of outlining and revising, but that's a sign your story (and its population) is coming alive. It may feel a bit nerve-wracking to allow your story to wander off, seemingly without you. But never fear, you're there. And you may find the best version of your story was the one that developed when your characters had a say in what exactly that story was.

> Here are some **FLASH EXERCISES** to do to get some thoughts going on conflicts. Answer these questions about your characters in relation to the world of your story, and in relation to each other. If you're not sure about any of that, make stuff up! Just a couple of sentences for each to get you started:
>
> Who/what are the character and conflict? You have a character and the person, thing, situation, or force that the character is up against.
>
> What does the person/thing/situation/force want from the character?
>
> What's the best possible outcome for this conflict?
>
> Who or what could deliver that outcome? The answer to this might be

something external to both the character and what they're in conflict with, or it might be the character themself who can make it happen.

Why would they do that for the character?

Why aren't they doing it?

What's the worst outcome to this conflict?

Chapter Eight

THE MEMORABLE SETTING CREATOR

YOU MIGHT THINK THAT WE'D TACKLE THE PLACE WHERE YOUR STORY UNFOLDS before we get to character, right? There's a method to that madness, I assure you!

Let's start with this: your readership doesn't know the landscape you're showing them. This is true whether they've been to the place in your story or not, down to the street your character lives on.

What do you think of when you think of setting? Maybe you think of the time or the place a writer chooses for their story. The story's setting can be a real time period or an identifiable, visitable location. It can also be a fictional world or an unfamiliar time (because it's not real, because it's ancient, because it's been bent and spun to suit the needs of the story). Setting can refer to the physical topography, the climate, the societal and cultural surroundings against which the action unfolds. It can be a world or one room. It can be crucial to your story, or purely incidental.

One thing I would suggest it should be, and that you should aspire to make it: a character all its own.

What do I mean by that? Consider the following sentiment from one of the very best authors:

> *"Place is where the quest for truth starts. A novel doesn't glow until its setting is accepted as true."* – EUDORA WELTY

Does this mean that every story, no matter what its organizing principle, its theme, its reason for existence, MUST have an extraordinary and memorable locale in order to work? No, it doesn't. Some stories are not dependent on the precise nature of their location to thrive, though there will still be setting-specific issues to address, like dialect, food, weather-appropriate clothes, etc. They take place in a small town, a big city, a cul-de-sac, and the author could use any such place without much noticeable difference. For those stories, as long as the cultivated world is believable, understandable, and consistent within its framework, they'll be fine. Create the map we talked about earlier, center your characters and the events on that map, and write away!

> "How your character feels about the setting is the key to making that setting memorable."

For other stories, setting is inseparable from the characters. It intertwines with them. It influences them and their actions. Their depiction is as deeply felt, as clear-eyed and attentive as the characters themselves. Can you imagine Harry Potter without Hogwarts? Gatsby without his mansion, or the pier, or the distant green light?

The place where your novel unfolds is more than just the backdrop of the story. It holds your characters' emotions and memories, whether by virtue of the characters hailing from that place, or because it stands in contrast to the place they come from. Around its corners are signposts and talismans your characters know intimately, or by the absence of those totems, the characters come to understand how far they've traveled from where they started. And so do we.

Like your characters, settings have a backstory. War took place there. Hard economic times have all but eliminated certain industries and the jobs they provided. They've borne witness to the passing of eras, the coming of new cultural landmarks, births, and deaths. Generations have grown up and moved away. Newcomers have arrived, looking to establish a home and roots. Like your characters, it's important to know the backstory, without regard to how much—if any—of that history makes its way into the story.

Setting is the ground upon which the characters walk, true. But it's also the ground they (and the very foundations of the story) rest upon.

So how can you make the setting vivid? How can you give life to the rich history of your setting when the setting isn't human? It has no voice, no mind with which to recount to the reader all that you might want to convey.

Consider this, perhaps one of the most profound bits of advice ever on writing:

"All description is an opinion of the world." – ANNE ENRIGHT

SETTING EXERCISE: Let me illustrate how to render setting vividly with an exercise. You'll need two other people to do this (don't worry, they don't have to be writers). Separate them so they don't hear the instructions.

Ask the first person to briefly, physically describe the room. The dimensions, the decor, the way the light looks, the color of the walls. A purely physical inventory of what they see around them.

Now, ask the second person to describe the same room, only add this: you've been in this room before. The last time you were here, something amazing—or horrible—happened to you. It was in this room that you found out you were about to be a new parent. It was here that someone proposed to you. In this room, in that chair looking at that wall or window, you were told you only had a few months of life left, or that someone you love had found another and was leaving.

Choose the mood, and ask them, with that in mind, to simply describe the room. The dimensions, the decor, the way the light looks, the color of the walls. A purely physical inventory of what they see around them.

Read these two descriptions, starting with the one that didn't have the experience attached to it. After you've read them both, ask yourself this: do you notice any difference between them? Is it attributable solely to the fact that two people can look at the same thing but choose different ways of describing it? Or do you notice an element in the second description that's missing from the first? A quality the second writer attributes to the colors, the light, the closeness of the walls, the quality of the air? Does that added dimension match the prompt you gave them about what happened the last time they were there? If the prompt referenced something joyful or exciting, is that the quality imbued in the colors and the furnishings and the way the light looks? Or does the room as described seem a bit melancholy, in keeping with the event you suggested to the second writer?

What just happened?

"All description is an opinion of the world."

In both iterations, there was only a room. The room was the same for both observers. Except it wasn't. In the second piece, the writer infused the setting not with details the other writer missed, but with a memory (created for the exercise) that informed how that setting came across.

In your story, the characters interact with their setting contextually. If they live in a big city, for example, how they view that city—its high-end neighborhoods, its tony restaurants, its exclusive clubs, and gleaming finery; or its gentrifying, suddenly out of reach dwellings, its haughtiness—is all in context to what extent they themselves are able to access that city. In other words, if two characters are walking down Michigan Avenue in Chicago, and one of them is well off and happy, while the other is struggling and alone, they're going to view the city in different ways. The city will *feel* differently to them, and relating that setting in your story, the streets, the storefronts, the passers-by, will reflect the context through which the characters see and experience it.

On writers' panels, I often tell the story of my first writing lesson on the subject of context. It came in the middle row of a downtown Chicago grindhouse theater, which I'd snuck into to see the Bruce Lee classic, *Enter the Dragon*. I was 11, and I sat in utter awe and amazement at what he could do. At the end, as the credits rolled, two older guys in the row behind me leaned forward and asked me what I thought. I probably babbled on a bit about what a miracle Lee was (I still feel this way).

"Totally agree," one of them said. "Such a shame he's dead."

I was stunned. Speechless. I didn't know.

And then, I sat through it again, on the spot. This time, as I watched him perform these feats, my mind kept a running dialogue in time to the scenes. *That's the last time he'll ever do that. He can't do that anymore. He's gone.*

When the music rose, the credits rolled and the screen went dark, it all meant something *else*. It had a finality to it. A poignance. And when I left the theater filled with the desire to see it again, it wasn't only because I loved it. It was because I wanted to bring him back, even for a few moments in a dark theater.

Two viewings of the same movie, one after the other. Two entirely different experiences. Why?

Because the *context* of that setting— a movie sparkling off the screen of an old theater in the heart of downtown Chicago, on a late Saturday afternoon in the childhood years of the character, first without, then with, a crucial bit of knowledge—made the same setting entirely different. The context came from the character.

The character's description of that moment changed because the character's opinion of the world changed, and when that happens, the setting reflects that.

Consider *The Great Gatsby* in light of what we're discussing: the way your characters' perceptions of the world are fueled by emotion, by social class, by economic and racial and gender-based inequity, by violence, by pure joy, by a sudden revelation—in other words, by any and all aspects of those characters' lives. Through Nick's eyes, we first notice Daisy's green pier light through his perception of Gatsby, standing in front of the house, fully immersed in the lush life that Nick admires. Gatsby is staring out over the water at that light, his arms "...stretched ... toward the dark water in a curious way, and, far as I was from him, I could have sworn he was trembling. Involuntarily I glanced seaward—and distinguished nothing except a single green light, minute and far away, that might have been at the end of a dock."

There's so much hope in Gatsby; after all, he's constructed his life—the real and unreal parts—from pure, sheer hope, that he can reclaim not only his lost love, but himself, as he was in those days. In this moment, the world before the two of them feels wondrous, the light a beacon of possibility. For Gatsby, an old love still burning for him. For Nick, the American dream of riches and status.

By the end of the novel, Gatsby's dream has taken a terrible and violent turn; his murder is equal in poignancy to the death of his dream as Daisy's life continues past the reality and the memory of him. As immersed as we are in this sharp rebuke of Gatsby's faith in the ability to recapture the past, we look once again through Nick's eyes at the world stretching to the foot of Daisy's dock and the green light:

"And as I sat there brooding on the old, unknown world, I thought of Gatsby's wonder when he first picked out the green light at the end of Daisy's dock. He had come a long way to this blue lawn and his dream must have seemed so close that he could hardly fail to grasp it. He did not know that it was already behind him, somewhere back in that vast obscurity beyond the city, where the dark fields of the republic rolled on under the night."

The same view, now described drastically anew. It stands in stark contrast to the warm glow that enveloped Gatsby's house, lawn, the water, and the far light, the first time the reader encountered them. They didn't change. The characters' perception of them did, and so the setting appears in an altogether different context.

Remember what we said at the beginning of this chapter? "Your readership doesn't know the landscape you're showing them. This is true whether they've been to the place in your story or not, down to the street your character lives on."

Why? Because while they may have visited the city your story takes place in, or walked through the town you spend time on, or bought many a meal from the real-life restaurant your plot point revolves around, your reader has never been to *your experience* of those places. They've never seen the street they grew up on filtered through anyone but themselves. They've never walked into a department store they thought they knew, only to discover it's completely transformed when perceived through the context of another human being.

Chapter Nine

THE SCENE CREATING ROADMAP

WALTER MOSELY SAID IT BEAUTIFULLY AND BEST: "Plot is the structure of revelation." As I think of this in my own writing, if story is what happens, plot is why it happens.

Let's consider the basics of a story outline:

> *The story premise*
> *The setting*
> *The characters*
> *The scenes*

That can feel like a lot if you've never tried to structure a novel, or memoir, or even a short story before. Even if you have, the question of *what am I trying to do with this idea* can be daunting, and writers can even feel blocked before they start. As we discussed at the very beginning of our work together, getting started involves consideration of that first sentence, the next, and the next, but also a general, vague notion of the overarching story, the events, and the time that passes. In other words, the things that happen even if you don't know where they happen, or when, or even whether they ought to.

Don't stop yourself before you start. Because as we stand here, at this point, you've been outlining this whole time!

At this point, you have a feel for the world you want to create—whether it'll come from pure imagination, from memory, from research, or from the view outside your front door. You have a sense of at least some of the characters. You also have a basic feeling about what may be in store for them at least a little ways up the road from where you think you'll begin. You may even have a scene or two in mind—you may not be sure where they'll go exactly, but when you think of your story and the people populating it, there's that one incident, that exchange of dialogue, or that sudden twist, that you can't let go of.

That's the basic framework of an outline. It might even be enough to get you started. But let's see if we can't sketch out the map of your story a bit more. Let's place them at the starting point of the story and plot their path toward the end. If this was a race, we're at the starting line. We know there's an end ahead of us. The key to truly inhabiting your outline, and therefore your story, is to take in all that you see between the start and the finish. It's good to keep at least a rough idea in mind of how it ends (and allow for that sense of an ending to change as the story progresses), but please do pay attention to the people, places, and moments you go through on your way. They may well become elements of the story, perhaps even critical ones.

You have options at your disposal when it comes to outlining. You can make it brief, like a synopsis. Against that bare skeleton of the story idea, you can write your way in and see where things lead. To some, this may feel like unfettered freedom. To others, though, this may be too anxiety producing and worrisome precisely because it's shorter and less filled in. Worry not—for you there's the other end of the spectrum. A highly detailed and lengthy outline form, which can feel in the end like a draft unto itself.

You can move through your outline chronologically, or you can draft the beginning and the end, then pick a side and work your way forward or backward from there. Remember, don't be afraid of changing the beginning or end (or both) depending on where the crafting of your story takes you. For me, the last page I write is almost always the first page of the novel. Only when I arrive at the end, and take note of all the story strands that brought me to that point, do I have a true sense of where the beginning ought to be.

At its heart, your outline is a blueprint of how you think the story might develop. It traces what happens and what happens next, all the way to the end. Try not to be afraid of including things that only just occur to you while outlining—those things you hadn't planned on or even thought of, that perhaps feel like they're hijacking the story and taking it in a direction you weren't expecting. You may use those tangents and notes, or not. Outlining is an exercise, much like the *pass it* game. It will steer you toward consideration of your story as something fluid and alive, full of possibilities worth exploring and, just maybe, worth trying.

Speaking of, remember the *pass it* game we played? Let's recap—in that exercise, you ask and answer basic questions as fast as you can (ten seconds or less), then move to the next. You can do this with a couple other people or a whole bunch of people. You can do this alone as well, though the spontaneity of someone throwing unexpected twists into the exercise really makes it fun.

> First person: Who is the character (physical attributes, emotional state, anything you think might be relevant)?...PASS!
>
> Second: Where are they (time/place)?...PASS!
>
> Third: At the moment the story opens, where are they in terms of story. What's happening?...PASS!
>
> Fourth: What's their conflict/problem?...PASS!
>
> Fifth: Make their problem worse...PASS!
>
> Sixth: Make their problem WAY worse...PASS!
>
> Last: FIX IT

That exercise is in fact built on German novelist Gustav Freytag's pyramid method, which added a couple of elements to the basic story elements originally conceptualized by Aristotle. Hey, just because I'm not MFA doesn't mean I don't know a few things!

As conceptualized in Freytag's pyramid, your outline covers these moments:

Exposition: The beginning of the story

Rising action: This is where tension enters the picture, usually fairly close to the beginning of the story. The stakes begin to rise as the story develops. Obstacles and conflicts appear. The first story point occurs roughly one-third of the way into the story. It sends the character(s) into the main conflict—the defining, the most critical desire or need, blocked by the key obstacle. This first story point is usually the first truly "big" moment of the story. It's what sets in motion all that comes after.

Around the midpoint, there's what's sometimes referred to as the first "pinch point." Your character's under the gun because of what happened at—or because of—the first story point. They have to make a decision. As a writer, you'll want to make clear both this decision and the consequences that flow from it. By this time in the story—the middle, approximately—that decision is made. Let the consequences flow!

After that, and as part of those consequences, a new plan emerges to deal with the pinch point and its consequences. All may seem hopeless in the formation and execution of this plan, leading to…

Climax: The high point

Falling action: After the climax but before the ending. It may well involve the consequences of the climax.

Resolution: The end!

Sound like a lot? You've already played with this structure: *pass it!*

Part of the *pass it* exercise involved identifying the problem (the conflict) and making it worse, worser, worsest (there's just something really satisfying about writing those non-words!), and then fixing it. In a nutshell, that's the "rising action/climax" portion of the pyramid. Whatever the conflict is, or the story's plan for your character(s), the midpoint should involve some degree of "'worse and worser." The odds should increase in opposition to what your characters are trying to achieve. The stakes rise. The obstacles increase in complexity or numerosity, as do the tasks (external or internal) your character has to do. The skills they must acquire, the actions they must undertake that they didn't think they'd have to do before. Old wounds have to be, at long last, faced and dealt with.

Your outline should place your characters, and by extension the story they live in, at risk. They find themselves in difficult spots. As the writer, this is job one. Lead them there even if it makes you uncomfortable. Even if you've no earthly idea how to resolve it, or how the character/you will extricate them from it. You may well surprise yourself with the solution that comes to you, even if it's hours, days, or weeks later.

THE WORSENING – HOW CAN I MAKE IT WORSE?

Here are some thoughts on how the story outline might make things worse for your characters:

Danger: This can be physical, mental, spiritual, or emotional. I know that these elements (rising action, climax) can sound like action story points, but even the very best literary writing, be it fiction, memoir, or even poetry, involves some degree of danger. Your character must face their own fears. They must confront a long-estranged family member. They must acknowledge that they'll never have the love they long for. They must seek treatment, at last, for the issue that's destroyed their life. All of this pertains to the character, and therefore the story, coming into contact with a dangerous element. By their nature, those elements move the character into unexpected, unwanted directions. How they respond—your outline and your story unfolds from that.

Bring in new faces: What do you do when you're not sure how to handle something? If you're like me, you try to get help from someone. Your character may need to do this too. Does that person already exist in your story? Are certain skills needed to address the story point, and does anyone already on the page (believably) possess that skillset? If not, a new character might enter, and with them, the unpredictability that comes along. Which is an exciting thing! Perhaps they're a "one-off," a character meant only to help your main character and story progress to the next event. Or maybe they stay on a bit longer. Maybe they become integral to the story itself. How do you know?

The answer is – start by writing one sentence summarizing your story. Then, expand it to address your main character, a few of the supporting characters, and the new one(s). Where do they start? Where do they end up? What's their purpose? Their motivation, goal(s), conflict(s)?

Ask yourself, is the story summary a bit different (beyond the immediate scene where that character is introduced) now that you know more about the characters including the new one? If the answer is yes, and the reason it's yes involves the new character as much as the existing ones, you may have yourself a character meant to play a greater role in the story. Keep them in mind as your outline moves forward. See if they pop up, naturally, in scenes that you may have conceived before they were around.

Obstacles: Obstacles can be in the present of your story—your character must reach her child across distance before something awful happens. They can arise from the past as well—a visit home triggers a long-buried trauma. The important thing is to make sure the reader never forgets why it's important that the character crosses the rope bridge, or has to get home by five, or has to face the reason they're unable to get past their depression. Don't let them or us linger in one spot for no reason.

Speaking of…

Stories move: Location to location, day to day, crisis to crisis, person to person, and so on. Nothing interesting generally happens when the story is in stasis, in real time or emotionally. As you look for the next thing that happens in your outline, make sure to ask yourself, where are they now, and where might they be next? How much time has (or should have) gone by when they go to the next scene?

These tips will help you navigate your story—the *what happens* of it all. But your outline should also reflect your developing sense of *why* it happens.

Chapter Ten

THE PLOT BLUEPRINT

LET'S REVISIT THAT GORGEOUS AND SO, SO TRUE STATEMENT FROM MR. MOSELY: "Plot is the structure of revelation."

To me, revelation of why things happen in your story occurs right alongside the story as it progresses. Think of it this way: your story, and the outline of those scenes that advance the story from its exposition to its resolution, is the world we see. We find out what the characters are like, where they are, what they do with the situations the story presents to them, what situations or circumstances they came from.

Your plot is the world revealed to us as we read. We learn things we didn't know. The story tells us that the characters left a place and headed elsewhere, but the plot tells us why they left. The story tells us what they do, but the plot tells us why they do it. Story tells us where they are, geographically and emotionally, and plot tells us why they're there. It tells us why they react the way they do. It fills us in on their past experiences, their traumas, their fears and strengths and abilities and how they acquired them, so we gain a deeper understanding of the *why* of it all.

Put another way, your plot lives in the spaces between story and pinch points. There are the actions that happen to your characters, and the actions they take in response, and the effect of those actions on the characters and their world. In between, there's the *why* of it all. The deepening. The small, closely observed experiences. The gestures and inabilities to speak to something, or handle an issue, or think things through rather than give in to anger or depression or unreasonable denial, that tell us what we need to know about these human beings facing human decisions. And please, don't lose sight of that: whether your story pits your characters against an invasion from outer space, or a repressive regime from a time long past, or a love relationship gone intransigently wrong, you're depicting people. Regular, fallible, uncertain, flawed, relatable people. People whose thoughts and actions tell us why *worse* got *worser*, and how they'll respond.

I hear what you're worrying about on the topic of outlines: what if you get stuck, and can't move forward with the outline? What if you get mired in concerns like "I still don't know how to get from A to B, from beginning to the next thing that happens, and on to the end. I just don't know what the structure of the story should be."

When those concerns are the loudest voice in your head writing-wise, it can be hard to get going. I've been there.

When that happens—and it's pretty much inevitable on any newly started piece—I like to take a deep dive into comparable works, analyzing their structure and arcs, across a swath of various authors' works.

Sound like a lot, right? It's actually simpler than you think.

I want to share with you one of the most efficient and effective lessons I ever learned. This exercise quite literally taught me how to think about structuring a novel from beginning to end. It taught me the techniques to employ and where/when to employ them. Most of all, it taught me that I could do it. So can you.

I call it the Blueprint Method. It goes like this:

Select a book or story that reminds you in some way of what you're writing (if after the foregoing steps you still have no idea, any book or story that you read and liked, or haven't read yet but want to, will do).

Now, read the first chapter. If it's a short piece, read it all. If you like, you can read it a page or two at a time (though you may find this approach a bit choppy). After you've completed that, ask and answer two simple questions:

Question one: What do I know?

This is where you jot down what's been communicated to you about the story so far. What's happening? Where is it? When is it? Who is it happening to? What do you know about them? What feeling are you getting about what may come?

Question two: How do I know it?

This is where you examine and catalogue the tools employed by the writer to get the things you noted in the first question across to you as a reader. What point of view did they use (first, second, third)? Is it in present tense or past? Did they use foreshadowing? If so, when and where in their telling of the story? Did they use flashbacks? If so, where/when? What's the tone? Is it serious? Snarky? Mournful? Are they using lush, flowery language, or is it spare and to the point? Is the author conveying a passage of time? How did they do it?

Repeat this exercise at the end of every chapter. When you've finished, you'll have a blueprint of the book. You'll see the writer's decisions. You'll see where and why the author used certain techniques. You'll see how they created time passages, shifts in perspective, introduction of new characters or plot points, resolution of conflicts. You'll have a map of the story, the paths the characters followed, and the ways the author did it. You just took a class in that author's work and significantly deepened your reading experience. In other words, you just read it like a writer.

"After each chapter, ask and answer two simple questions: what do I know; and how do I know it?"

Do this again with another book, and another. Before long, you'll have a survey of multiple strategies authors employed to use all the same writing tools you're acquiring now. POV, flashbacks, character plot arcs. You'll begin to see differences and the similarities in the ways they construct their stories.

Having done this, now you'll go back to your outline. Break it down into its components—the beginning scenes, the middle ones, the end. As you go through each section, ask yourself, what do I know? At this point in the story, is that enough to know? Should I know more by this point? Less? How do things change from scene to scene? How do the characters change?

You can ask yourself as well, how do I know what I know? What might I use to convey that information? Will I use first person or third? Will I drop a digression into a character's past at this point in the narrative? Should I foreshadow an event at the end of a chapter?

For many of these questions, you'll know how to answer *"how do I know it"* after you write your way in. If you want to get to know a character, write them (as we've done extensively to this point). If you want to know how a particularly thorny, seemingly intractable conflict might turn out, write your way to it, making full use of the characters you've come to know and how they'd handle adversity of any kind, how they are in emotional situations, and the setting you've brought to vivid life. By the time you get there, you'll likely have an idea.

But—and I fully get this—there are issues that can weigh on us. The inability to answer them with confidence can leave us feeling insecure and block us from moving forward. It's like walking through a strange doorway into a pitch-black room. We don't like that uncertainty. We want to know what we're getting into ahead of time.

Now, I can't fully free you from that uncertainty, or how it feels when it hits. It's something universal among us writers, and one we can only truly answer for ourselves by entering our story, inhabiting it, and setting out in as compelling a way as possible what happens. There are some universal bumps in all our roads. Let's think about some ideas for how to get around, over or through them, starting with one I hear about all the time from fellow writers. Like the blueprint method hopefully illustrated for you, there's no one surefire way to get where you're going. There is, though, the best way for you, and that's the one that matters. So let's look at some of the most common questions all writers of all forms and genres encounter.

Chapter Eleven

THE WRITER'S BLOCK DISRUPTORS

FLASHBACKS AND NARRATIVE SUMMARIES – *How do I know when to use them? How do I avoid overuse?*

A flashback, or narrative summary, takes the reader out of the story's "present" (whenever that may be taking place) and into the past of the characters (flashback) or into their heads so we can be told how they feel and why (narrative summary) in order to reveal something. Motives, past experiences, formative events in their lives; things that provide greater context and revelation to the present situation they find themselves in. These are used widely in storytelling, from television to film, from novels to memoir to poetry. I have a personal favorite use of flashback from the classic film *Enter the Dragon*. We're introduced to each of the three main characters—Lee, Roper and Williams—as they make their way to the ship that will take them to Han's island and the martial arts tournament that forms the central setting of the story. Each of them gets their own personal flashback, complete with an eddying wash over the screen to signify we're leaving their present. We see what happened to each of them (the death of Lee's sister, Roper's gambling debt to the mob, Williams' run-in with racist police) that launched their respective journeys. It may not be literature, but for this eleven-year-old, it was a formative introduction to flashback usage.

A famous structure for flashback can be found in the timeless film *Sunset Boulevard*. The story is actually told entirely in flashback, opening at a mansion on the titular street as a group of police officers and photographers discover the body of Joe Gillis, floating face down in the swimming pool. In a flashback that spans the length of the film, Joe relates the events leading to his death. We end where we began, poolside, watching his lifeless body float.

This is an extreme use of flashback, and can be considered a kind of pact with the reader. The story begins with a high point and goes backward in time. The author has made a promise to the reader: stay with me, there's an explanation for this that will make this compelling image all the more so.

In a sense, a story that's told in past tense by a palpable, tangible narrator makes this promise. The reader knows via this technique that the narrator is telling the story from some present time, and we follow them back in history to where things started, knowing that by the time we get to the end of their remembrance, their journey will have taken on greater meaning and resonance.

In fiction, flashbacks interrupt the chronological progression of the story. They return to an earlier time to illuminate the present and provide critical information about it. They can be accomplished via quick glimpses or longer sections within the narrative. Either way, it's best to use them sparingly; after all, by definition they interrupt the forward momentum of the story.

Flashbacks can achieve a number of goals. They help character development. They bring other time periods into the story. They connect the readers to the characters on a deeper level (the bad guy recalling earlier abuse, for example). They explain the current conflict in a more vivid way, avoiding long monologues about how everything came to the state things are in as the readers join the story. Long histories of bad blood between warring factions, as an example; it's likely far more interesting to experience the past in active passages than to be told about them by a tribal elder, right? Yet, if the story as it's structured wouldn't benefit from starting way back in time, a well-placed flashback will provide great illumination of that troubled past.

Narrative summaries ideally present the character's thoughts in a way that reflects their traits (kindness, surliness, generosity, selfishness). They can come into play when the author wants to cover a lot of time, or a lot of plot, in a small space. They ought not be used as a tool to present backstory, but you'll see that sort of misuse frequently. They're not showing, but telling.

Flashbacks and narrative summaries can be overused. Your story will almost always benefit from spending the majority of its narrative in real time—in scenes where we are with the characters as they experience something, rather than be told about it. Let's look at this a bit more closely.

A scene is in real time, in an identified location (geographic and in terms of time), and involves dialogue or action between those present. A narrative summary, on the other hand, describes or "tells" about an action or conversation, but doesn't show it. One way to think about it: deciding whether something should go into a presently, fully told scene vs. a flashback or narrative summary involves issues of tension and pacing.

- Is the event or information significant enough to the story to warrant a full scene?
- Does it move the story forward?
- Does it lead the character toward a turning point or plot point, preferably both, that you want the reader to remember and experience along with the character?
- Are the events action or reaction? In other words, is something happening, or are the characters making decisions based on something that has already happened?
- If it is action, does it directly impact the POV character, and are you giving them an opportunity to react to it?
- Is there identifiable conflict between two characters, between what your main character wants and what they need, or preferably both?
- Are you providing important information that a reader is likely to skim over, misunderstand, or not care about in narrative form? Remember, the reader doesn't know what you know–that it's important.

If the answer to any of those questions is yes, you may not want to use narrative or flashback. Aim straight for what it is that's making the character—and, perhaps, you as the writer—uncomfortable. Explore it in real time. That's where the story will be at its most vivid, as will your experience of writing it.

Shifting away from the story's present to a past moment or incident that reveals something relevant to that present situation can be effective if used sparingly and strategically. Overuse, though, will leave your readers with feelings of "don't leave now" and "don't avoid this moment" as the narrative drops in a summary of a past event. The impact of this will be felt in the story, in the form of too much distance from the characters and the plot.

Overuse can also lead to another issue: avoidance. As you draft your story (and particularly in revisions, which we'll get to), make particular note of those scenes where the character (and you) feel uncomfortable, anxious, afraid of the moment and its consequences. Do you see any pattern of sudden shifts in those scenes to flashback or summary? You may be avoiding the situation. Lean into it—those feelings are why you're writing, to explore them, and they're certainly why your readers will keep turning pages.

If it seems to you that you may be overusing either or both of these techniques, try this: outline your characters' stories separately. Beginning to end, as if they were the main character and the only POV from whom the entire story emerges. What happens in each scene? Are we present for it, or are we told about it? Do we see, in real time, the disruption of their lives because of a clear, unavoidable conflict, the gathering/acquisition of needed information or skills to address that conflict, the trying and failing and trying again to overcome it, and the overcoming (or, perhaps, the "learning to co-exist with it")? In those scenes where narrative summary/segues/flashbacks take the reader away from the issue, pull it into the present. Write that portion as if it was happening to them now.

Some additional tips on making good use of flashbacks and narrative summaries:

VERB TENSE

If the flashback is a short one, a brief description works just fine. But if a longer digression is needed, which will mean a break in the story's present in order to go as deeply as the story requires, and the book is written in past tense already, you can use past perfect to clearly delineate the transition.

Imagine that your character flies to Paris to pursue the love of her life. The story is written in past tense ("she boarded the plane clutching her passport..."), and now you want to drop a flashback in that explains why your character is so apprehensive. Past perfect will signify the departure from the book's present ("she had been to Paris before..."). After a few sentences in this verb tense, the reader will adjust to the new timeframe and you can return to past tense until the end of the flashback digression, at which time you can transition out to your story's present again.

RELEVANCE

Flashbacks should be only as long as they need to be, and contain only what they need to. I know, that's pretty vague! A good rule to follow: the flashback should give the reader what they need in order to understand, on a deeper level, the moment/place/person/conflict point we were at when the departure to the past takes place. Keep in mind that in your characters' present (the place we're leaving to visit this past event), life is still going on. In other words, if the house is ablaze and they're choking on the smoke, is that the right time to leave them for a digression into how they came to the neighborhood? No matter how interesting that story may be, now's most likely not the time.

The story moves forward. The characters' remembrances move backward. They meet at resonant points along the way. What does that mean? Let's look at a short story for an example.

Imagine this scenario: a young woman returning to her hometown after a long and unexplained absence to be at her father's bedside as he passes. The present story consists of her father's death in the hospital, followed by a gathering at the home of her grandfather. As she keeps a vigil over his increasingly labored breathing and weakening heartbeat, she muses on their lives and the family dynamics. That's a rich vein for flashbacks that take us out of that stifling room and into the forces that shaped their relationship. In one or the other of the present settings (the room and the house in which his death is marked with a memorial gathering of family and friends), that's where the memories you place throughout the narrative will come to meet her where she is. She may think back to her childhood, and through that rumination, we learn something about her and the situation at that time. How will that further illuminate, expand, and amplify her present life for the reader? If they were estranged, for example, a memory of an incident in which the estrangement's seeds formed would give her present story more resonance and meaning.

That's the first of two front-and-center questions for each such memory you drop into the narrative. The second question is, is there a better place for the memory to go in search of the story's present? In this piece we're using as a hypothetical, the memories have two places to find her: bedside with her father, or at her relatives' house. Is that her childhood home or a place she spent a lot of time in? Perhaps a memory returning to her might find her in front of a familiar window view, or a photo of her father, or something representative of the time the memory springs from, like a memento of a car trip or an argument that shattered a childhood illusion of her family.

TELL THE PRESENT STORY FIRST

When in doubt—when the uncertainty over where to drop a flashback digression overtakes you and causes you to feel stuck—write your draft in chronological fashion (or in whatever mode of telling you decided on). Don't worry about specific flashback usage, but do keep a pad of paper near, and when that feeling begins to tug at you, that "You know, maybe here would possibly be a spot to say something more about why she's feeling this way," jot that down. The spot in the story where you felt that you might want to digress. When you revise, you'll have a map (I know—I like my maps!) of flashback possibilities. You'll also have a more complete sense of story, and with that a better sense of where a flashback might help illuminate things. It will be clearer to you, among the story's various twists and turns, where a flashback may make sense to place.

TRIGGER

As I noted above, there should be a reason why your characters enter a flashback (or the unnamed narrator, the omniscient POV, digresses away from the moment to bring the reader back to a past event). It does constitute a pause in the forward progress of the story, so sparing use is a good thing. Keep that analogy in mind: we likely wouldn't pause and remember how we came to the neighborhood in the middle of a raging house fire… unless, perhaps, the character is lying on the floor, dying of smoke inhalation, and their life is flashing before their eyes, but even then, do we really want to step away from the intensity of the scene? Like anything else, that's a decision for you, the writer to make. Whether it's the right one will depend wholly on what best serves the story.

Considering the trigger is always important in flashback placement. Ideally, the flashback will simultaneously inform the reader of context and illuminate and deepen the moment in the story that the reader just left. Take, as an example, a truly perfect film. No, not *Enter the Dragon* (though it is perfect, and I'll hear no arguments). No, I'm talking about *Casablanca*. Out of nowhere, Ilsa reappears in Rick's life—the trigger. He gets drunk and remembers key events from his past that broke his heart—the flashback. Late in the film, having returned to a past Paris with him, we understand the depth of his heartbreak, and of his sacrifice, when he tells her to get on that plane with her husband. "We'll always have Paris" packs a hell of an emotional wallop, one that would have been significantly lessened had we just been told about it, rather than stepping back in time via flashback and immersing ourselves in their time together before the Nazi invasion tore them apart.

WRITER'S BLOCK

If you find yourself pausing mid-scene because a question occurred to you and you don't know how the issue plays out in the moment you've created, it means your story and your characters are starting to speak to you. They're suggesting that in a situation you may have outlined for them before you even met them on the page, they might do something other than what you intended. Your story is coming alive.

Try thinking differently about that block. It's not just "I can't write, this is garbage, I'm stuck, I don't know where to go after this..."

That block is also valuable data.

Some writers think of writers' block from the outside in; that is, the issue arises because of something outside us that we can't control. Distractions, our own inability, or inexperience. Others think of it from the inside out—a problematic turn of events in the story or a blind alley we've wandered down and don't know how to get out of. While I mostly adhere to the latter—the issue is almost always in the story, not the world outside of it—I have a different take as to why we as writers can sometimes come to a blockage and not have any idea what to do about it.

Writer's block, like beta reader feedback—the sensation that something's not working—is certainly anxiety producing, but it's important to remind yourself that feeling blocked isn't fatal. It's like an error message on your computer. It's meaningless to all but those who speak code. You speak your novel. You KNOW it. With some pointers and suggestions on things to consider, you'll be able to turn those vague "it's not quite working" sensations into meaningful action plans for attacking your story, whether it's a first draft or a final revision.

Let's figure out how to read the message that block is sending. First, what triggered the error message? Apathy, perhaps? That feeling that you have no creative spark to give to your work? Anger, maybe? You might be experiencing feelings about your writing not gaining the sort of notice you wanted. Perhaps you're comparing yourself to other writers, ones you know or don't know, and perhaps their experience with publishing, selling, public readings, posts that draw lots of admiring comments and likes, has taken up residence inside you. Don't worry, we all feel that envious sensation sometimes! Compare and despair, as the saying goes.

Maybe it all comes down to good old anxiety. Are you familiar with "imposter syndrome"? That persistent doubting of your own abilities? Ever feel like a fraud about your abilities as a writer, or a professional within your chosen career niche, or as a parent, partner, friend? It can absolutely affect people trying to achieve something, who then find it difficult to accept their own accomplishments. Many question whether they're deserving of any accolades at all.

If you see any of this at the heart of your inability to get started, or to move past a block during your writing, here are a few tips:

1. Take a break! It really helps to step away from your writing and get some air, a change of scenery, a fresh perspective. Writers have it in our heads that to *be* writers, we need to chain ourselves to the desk and stare into the cold light of our laptops (I'm a pad and pen kind of writer, but you get my meaning) for days on end. There are certainly times when you get into a flow. Hours go by and they seem like mere moments. You look at what you've done, and you marvel at the amount and at that extraordinary feeling of timeless suspension inside the moving parts of your story. Rejoice in that feeling! But recognize it's not going to be your daily experience. There will be plenty of times when you'll be grinding for each word. Those are the "butt in chair, word on page" days. But that's as much *writing* as the feeling of flying, or of being stuck, is also *writing*. In all those moments, remind yourself that when you're writing, you're doing the work, and when you're thinking about your story or your characters and the roads they'll travel, you're doing the work too! So, if you feel a bit stuck, clear your head. Take a walk. You may surprise yourself— some obvious solutions and ideas come while you're humming a song or thinking about a favorite moment in someone else's story.
2. Jump to a section of your story that you feel good about. That's not ducking the hard parts. Doing this forces you to consider where the story has been and where it ought to go (and it forces you to consider if those are different directions), in relation to the part you're stuck on. That, in turn, will help you reassess what's happening in that moment you can't quite get past.
3. Go back to the beginning and read. It's another way to clarify what's gone before, to get you where you now find yourself. It's also a way to surprise you, depending on how far in you may be when you pause to do this. I often have that feeling of "oh, I wrote that?" when I go back to the beginning.
4. Freewrite, as we covered earlier. Get those creative impulses flowing!
5. Talk to a friend: Whether you have someone to talk to or you just talk to yourself, "tell a friend" what's happening in your story. Tell it out loud— here's what the book is about, and here's what happens first, next, next… You can do this in the form of a letter to yourself as well. When you get to the part that you're having difficulty with, take particular note of how you're trying to describe it to that "friend."

6. Remind yourself that you, and only you, truly know this story. You know how to tell it, or else it wouldn't have found you. Don't let yourself get too frustrated about the "stuckness" you're experiencing.

None of the above feel quite right to you? What else might it be?

Some other common issues:

Perhaps your story is more premise than plot. A great idea is a wonderful thing, but it takes more than a premise to create a plot. Many novels fail because all they are is a premise.

For example, "Four siblings go through a magical wardrobe into another world" is a concept with lots of potential, but there's no plot to be found. It's what the siblings do once they get to that magical world that creates the plot, and the magic, that is *The Lion, The Witch and The Wardrobe*. As we've discussed, the characters' decisions determine how a plot unfolds. That's where your intimate knowledge of the characters comes into play. You know what they'd do. Don't be afraid to let that knowledge guide where the plot goes.

Perhaps there aren't enough choices. The more choices you give a character, and the harder you make those choices, the more unpredictable the plot (and the story's outcome) will be. Each tough choice should have consequences attached to it: punishments for failure and reward for success. There should be stakes hanging over the character.

Or maybe it's all in your protagonist's head.

Stories that are too internal and focus too much on how a character feels and thinks often lack a solid plot because there's nothing for the character to actually do.

For example, if the protagonist's goal is to "be happy," there's no direction to help you create the plot. But if the goal is to "find a higher-paying job and move out of his parent's basement," you have clear steps the protagonist can take and choices he can make to create his next move, and the next.

It could be that there's no one or nothing worth fighting for. Stories are only as strong as their antagonists, and a weak antagonist makes for a weak plot. The antagonist (be it a person, society, or nature) creates the obstacles the protagonist will need to overcome to succeed. That may be the way around your obstacle. He, she, or it sets the conflict in motion and presents the first choice the protagonist will have to make. Which in turn makes the antagonist react and make a choice, forcing another protagonist choice and another action and so on until the climax. Based upon your knowledge of the characters, you'll know how they'll react to each set of circumstances.

Which leads me to that different take I mentioned. Of course the reasons for feeling blocked that I listed above may absolutely be at play in your situation. But if I may, let me suggest what may really be going on, and what is, for me, always the first place I start.

It's not a block.

You're not "stuck," whatever that may mean. What's happening is, your characters are telling you that they wouldn't do what you've outlined and planned for them to do. They've changed, and they're trying to get your attention. What's happening is simply that you don't know your characters well enough to trust them in situations or story arcs. You feel uncertain about what to do because you feel uncertain about what *they'd* do. It just may be that you don't know your character well enough yet to know their opinion about the world you've set them in.

If this resonates, go back to our character arc exercises, our "yellow light game," and spend a bit more time with them. Put them in situations outside the story, then ask, "What would they do?" Now, transfer that increased knowledge of them to your story. What will they do in that moment that you stopped at?

Chapter Twelve

REWRITE SECRETS

IF YOU'VE COME THIS FAR, YOU'VE JUST COMPLETED A FULL DRAFT OF your novel, short story, story collection, or memoir. Congrats! If you've done all that AND you've now turned immediately to this section on revising said work, damn! You go-getter, you. Do me a favor: set your work, and this book, aside for a while. A week at least, perhaps two. Write something else, if you're feeling it. Take a break if you're feeling a bit tired, or a bit spent, or even a bit worried about what you just finished writing. Read—always an incredibly valuable recharge source. Engage in actual conversations with others when your mind isn't at least partially immersed in the work. Get some rest, some recreation, and most important, some distance between you and what you've written.

And, of course, recognize the accomplishment! It's huge, what you just did. Go celebrate, and come back fresh.

As hard as it can be to do, on that first draft you hopefully turned the editor side of your brain off. You just wrote. You put as much down as you possibly could. Warts, mistakes, false moves, blind alleys, scenes that felt clunky as you wrote them and dialogue that no one in real life would ever say. You (hopefully) typed it all in and went right on to the next section and the next, and you (hopefully) told yourself "I'll get it on the rewrite." Because you will.

It's so hard to turn that editing function off, isn't it? Dwelling over a sentence that you know could be better is easier than staring down the road at an uncertain end point, or around the corner at a scene to come that you're not quite sure how to approach. That editor-on-your-shoulder is hard to dislodge sometimes. It's ok, we all have one. It pops up at inopportune moments and can derail our momentum. But we learn, if not to turn it all the way off, to tune it out a bit more each writing session.

But now you've arrived at that moment you promised yourself you'd wait for, before allowing the editor back in the room. This phase is every bit as creative as the initial draft phase was. Revising isn't all spellcheck and syntax, though we'll get there.

Some things about this phase that you may well experience for yourself:

YOU'LL SPEND MORE TIME IN THIS PHASE OF WRITING THAN IN THE INITIAL DRAFT

Make peace with that—this is truly where the majority of the work awaits you. I know that might sound a bit daunting, especially after all you've come through to get started, structure your story, get to know your characters, and guide the whole enterprise to its end. We'll walk through this phase together, and do keep in mind: you have a completed draft! The materials you need to sculpt your story are either right there before you, or absolutely suggested by what you've already written.

I've come to trust in a simple truth: the answer to the problem with my writing is almost always on the page, waiting for me to see it. Once you've reached the end of the first draft, all that time spent with the characters and their stories will pay off for you. You'll see what you've done—what THEY'VE done—in a much different way. That's the wellspring your revision will come from.

FOCUS.

Will the focus of your revision be about the story? Will it be about the quality of the writing? Will it be large pieces that need to be reordered or rethought? Will it be detail work, word by word?

The answer is "yes." It may be about all of these things. That may seem overwhelming, but recall that the notion of getting started, with that expanse of empty screen/pages before you, felt the same way. Remember?

Generally, the passes you make through your manuscript (yes, there will be more than one) start in a bigger-picture way, as we'll see below when we get into structuring and strategizing your revision work. I've found that the drafts following the first one start with story and move through successive passes all the way down to language as the story takes its final shape and my focus turns to the way the sentences flow one to the next, the transitions and the voice of the piece. That order may shift a bit when you transition your revision from yourself to an outsider such as a beta reader, an editor, or a workshop.

BE OPEN TO CHANGE, EVEN RADICAL CHANGE.

I know we've covered this before, but writing is an act of faith, of love, of truth-telling, and of bravery. As the extraordinary Annie Dillard said about the writing life: "This is why some writers say it takes courage to write. It does. Over and over you must choose the book over your own wishes and feelings."

All the attributes you bring to your writing, even the ones you didn't realize you possessed, will be on display when you hit that moment when you realize that a section of the story just isn't working. It doesn't fit, no matter all your herculean efforts to stuff it into the larger picture. A character, having developed through that first draft, went so far afield as to belong to a completely different story. A different character, one that doesn't even exist in your first draft, just let you know they belong in the new draft.

You know what? Maybe they do!

My second novel, *The Night Language*, changed rather dramatically somewhere between the third and fourth draft. A character was introduced ever so briefly in the second draft, aboard a ship bearing the main character, Alamayou, from Abyssinia to London and a new life he couldn't imagine. That minor character saw Alamayou across the ship's mess; their eyes met briefly because that minor, nameless character—like Alamayou—was black. They were the only such men aboard.

In the next draft, the character saw him not in the mess, but on deck, at the ship's rail. They speak briefly, their hands resting on the wood next to each other, and something unspoken passes between them. Their hands, alongside each other, resemble each other in a way that will be impossible for Alamayou to find in the unimaginable city he's traveling to.

That minor character became Philip in the next draft — the love of Alamayou's life. The story was completely, irrevocably altered, and it's that story that led to the novel's publication and positive reviews. Alamayou's journey was altogether different when Philip asserted his place in the novel and in the lives of Alamayou, Queen Victoria, her children, and the story's past and present. When the realization came that this change needed to happen, it came with a good deal of anxiety and even resentment at how much work I had ahead of me. Quite literally, no section of the novel would go unscathed if I worked this revision through from beginning to end, as I knew I needed to.

But I did it, and it made the difference between the story I had and the one that sold.

As I write this, I'm revising my new novel. I jettisoned over 150 pages of the first draft, because I knew I'd started with the wrong person. When I say jettisoned, I mean from the novel itself. I'll retain those pages separately, as I suggest you do with whatever you excise from your work. Those pages may yield something of real value, to the work you cut them from or to a future piece. You never know what even one sentence might lead you to. Just think about how we generated your idea, or brought it further out of the dark into a structure you then followed. Often, it's a mere kernel that sparks a whole flurry of ideas and possibilities.

WHEN IN DOUBT, DELETE.

Does the material you're evaluating (for inclusion or exclusion) during the revision phase move the story forward in an illuminating and productive way, or is it there because you really needed to say it…or really like the way you said it?

We can be honest with each other, right? We all write *those* sentences. The ones that just ring so beautifully, that carry the fullness of our experience, that say everything about the story in understated, pitch perfect prose (or at least *we* think so). But those beautifully wrought words don't fit the story, or the character, and upon making our way through the revision to the moment we read them, we know it. And if we know it, it's quite likely that the audience—editors, agents, readers—will know it too.

Time to bid those lovely words a fond farewell. By all means keep them someplace separate, as noted above. If your gut is telling you they don't quite ring right, trust that feeling and, in the immortal words of Arthur Quiller-Couch, who spread it in his widely reprinted 1913-1914 Cambridge lectures "On the Art of Writing": *kill your darlings.*

Aside: that quote has been attributed, variously, to Faulkner, Wilde, Ginsberg, Chekhov, Welty, and a host of others.

GET IN; GET OUT.

In each scene you revise, look for the quickest way into it, and then out of it. Although we writers are always looking to paint pictures for our readers, often a little detail carries the scene quite far enough. If you think of the setting of the scene as a car the characters are in, ask yourself, "It may be necessary, for the reader to truly feel this moment, to describe the type of car, or the color of the interior. But how much do they really need to know about every component of the engine?"

In other words, a lot of extraneous description—especially when you're past the initial exposition all stories have so the readers can ground themselves in time, place, and story—will likely act as a drag on the forward momentum of the plot. If you don't really need to walk with your character each step to the room where the actual scene will play out, just put them in the room. Likewise, it's not necessary (most of the time) to describe how they walk to the door, take hold of the handle, pause a moment, and so forth. This is figurative, of course; the point is, if there's nothing gained by freighting your scene with details and actions that don't relate directly to what the scene is looking to accomplish, cut them.

"COMPLETION FEAR"

The eminent author Margaret Atwood speaks of something all writers can relate to: that gnawing anxiety around the notion of actually finishing your story. The questions that can stymie you as you tackle the task of polishing, revising, and readying it for release into the wild. What if it's no good? What if the story is fine, but I'm just not a good enough writer to tell it as well as it deserves? What if no one cares?

For one thing, remember that no one sees your work until you say so. For another, feel free to make the same amount of missteps, mistakes, and underbaked writing as you did on the first draft. You can always change it. You're in revision—there's going to be more than one draft.

In the end, though, there's really only one piece of advice that you should take as hard truth: finish it anyway. Push through. Don't let the anxiety stop you. You've come this far. The only way you could have achieved what you have is by braving waters that made you uncomfortable, that caused you to doubt your abilities or your worthiness. Take this in, and keep reminding yourself (or work with me—I'll happily remind you): your story matters. The fact that you're telling that story matters. What matters just as much, if not more: it's your story, and that means you're the only one who can tell it. Don't stop. Seek connection and commiseration with other writers, with friends, but don't stop.

Let's talk about the nuts and bolts of revision.

THE BLUEPRINT METHOD, PART DEUX

Just as we used this method to create an outline for our first draft, we can and should run it back for round two and beyond. Recall that at the end of each chapter of a piece, we asked and answered two questions: what do I know, and how do I know it? So, how do we apply this to our own writing, now that we have a completed draft?

We read our work chapter by chapter, and then we ask and answer the same two questions. What does the reader know, based upon what we just read, and how does the reader know it?

Now, add a third question to this chapter-by-chapter study of your story. Can you guess what it is?

Yep. *Why?*

As you go back through your story in preparation for the revision, ask yourself at the end of each chapter, "Why did that happen? Why are the characters doing that? Why did the story go in that direction?"

You can probably see the subtext to those questions. For every "why" you ask, the next question should always be "Why that and not something else?" Does the choice you made for the story, or the choice made for the characters (or, at this juncture, the choice you suspect the characters are trying to make for themselves) make sense? Is there a better one? Is there a better way to portray the one you did make?

Now, to be sure, your answer to this question may well be "No, this is the right move at the right time. It advances the story, illuminates the characters and their reasons, and it rings true against the world I've created." In which case, move on to the next chapter. Revising your work doesn't necessarily mean that each and every event, scene, character, arc or plot point needs a teardown. Maybe they just need some tweaking. Maybe more. Maybe nothing at all. I would suggest that the latter is going to be more applicable to later drafts, as you get closer to your finished story. In the early goings, you can expect to see things that made sense at the time you wrote them, but don't work as you read them now. Perfect! That's what this phase is all about.

Now, have you noticed the one element that everything you'll encounter when revising have in common?

You.

The points above, and the game plan for revision to come, all contemplate you—and not an outside editor—doing the revision. Usage of outsiders will come, but at this point in your writing and revising journey, I do recommend that you take a shot at the task. Two or three rounds at least before you hand it off to that editor, or a writers' group, or beta readers.

Why?

For one thing, freelance editors can be expensive (myself included). They can charge anywhere from $.03 to $.05 per word or more. If you're handing them a novel that's in the preferred word count range—say, ninety thousand words—you're looking at between $2,700-$4,500 for a full and professional manuscript edit. If you have it to invest in yourself, a deep dive by an experienced writer/editor who will review your work with an eye toward what's best for the story, the characters, and the story's prospects out in the world, I can't recommend this route highly enough. But if I may, I still suggest you take the first couple of revision rounds on yourself.

Again, why?

Because I truly believe, and have personally experienced, that it makes us better writers. Think of how far we've come together through the generation and honing of your story idea, to plot and character, setting and outlining. Going through those phases from novel to novel, I feel the improvements each time and that goes double for revising those very elements. Follow me through the revision game plan below, and see if it doesn't leave you feeling the same way.

A word about something we just touched on: outside readers.

That first draft you hold is very, very close to your heart. It's also, in all likelihood, not ready for others to see no matter how we might feel. As we discussed previously, when we hand over our writing to anyone except that certain loving family member or friend—you know the one, your ride or die, neither-of-you-can-do-wrong-in-each-others'-eyes individual who will assure you that you're great no matter what's actually on the page—they're doing you no favors whatsoever by telling you only what you want to hear.

Most of the time, when you hand something over to a reader, you're going to hear what's wrong with it. Perhaps, more than you expect, and more than you're prepared for. Discouragement is painful for all of us. It can leave us feeling, at best, uncertain how to proceed, and at worst, uncertain whether proceeding is even worth it (pro tip: expressing the story that's been waiting for you to find it is ALWAYS worth it).

There's no need to put yourself through that at an early-draft stage. By the time you've put in more writing work via revision, and see for yourself not only what needs attention but what's possible, what's inherent and vital and emerging in that beauty you've created, you'll be far more ready and able to receive feedback. As new to writing as you may be—at least, writing with an eye toward representation and even publication—let me assure you of something that all of us, as writers, need to be reminded of.

You are the boss of your work. You know best what you're trying to do. This is really, truly, yours. That's why they're called "beta" readers. The alpha is you. So trust that same mind and heart, the one that dreamt of this story, turned the story over and over in that mind, shed sweat and tears and blood to realize that story, to now pull the story out and refine it. Remember, the first draft is the gathering of stone. Now it's time to carve until the art emerges.

You can do it and I'm here to help!

Ready for a game plan? Let's go.

THE GAME PLAN

Ok. You've completed your first draft, set it aside and done something else. Perhaps a few something elses. You stepped away and are now coming back to your story feeling fresher and not quite so intimately entwined with it.

To be sure, you may have a crystal-clear idea of what needs to be done. Perhaps as you wrote the first full draft, you kept a running series of observations and notes on what you need to do in the rewrite. I do that, and I find it extremely helpful, as by the time I reach the end, I may not remember what it was I thought might be needed or where that issue arose in the manuscript.

Maybe, though, you're not sure how to approach the revision. Here are several revision strategies you can think about trying, from the big picture down to the small details.

Let's start with the big picture.

THE HIGH LEVEL PASS

Some folks use index cards for this pass (a review of the full manuscript), but a simple pad or separate document will do nicely. Beginning with the first chapter, create a chart of developments. This isn't the time to read for story, or for sentence structure or word choice. All you want to do right now is, from one chapter to the next, create a simple chronological chart of what happens, what happens next, what happens after that, and so on. Do this all the way to the end for the main plot, then go back to the beginning and do it over for the subplot(s). Keep track of time passages between chapters, dates, and background events.

You can do this as well for each character, but if you're charting developments, the characters and their respective arcs will be among your notes. If you don't track this, you may want to go back to the beginning once again for your main and key supporting characters. You can't do too much of this, so no worries!

When that's done, lay it all out side-by-side. You'll be able to track, at a high level, how events move from chapter to chapter, how characters evolve from chapter to chapter, where the conflicts arise, where the world against which the story takes place comes in (and where it doesn't), and where the action is flowing vs. where it feels forced or not as present as it ought to be. Do the events move well? Does time pass smoothly and believably? Are there sudden leaps in plot or chronology? Do the characters evolve believably, or do they suddenly change from who the reader (or you, as the writer) thought they were without sufficient context or explanation for that change?

Mark those spots in the story that, for whatever reason, may need work. The questions that you want to ask yourself as you examine your draft at this juncture:

- *Do I need to cut any scenes or characters?*
- *Do I need to add any scenes or characters?*
- *Do I need to change any scenes or characters?*

Answer these only with your high-level chart.

If you think you do need to add/cut/change, or even if you're not sure, take the time to draft and/or revise those scenes now. You may not use them, or you may only use a portion.

Once you've drafted them, integrate them into the story.

When that's done, let's come down from a high-level, big-picture view to something a bit closer.

THE BREADCRUMBS PASS

Recall our work on getting started, outlining, and getting into the actual writing of that first complete draft. During that initial phase (ah, remember those heady days?), we noted the unique, alternately wondrous and scary feeling of the characters taking their narratives over. They start telling you that the direction you intended for them doesn't quite fit with who they've become or what they'd naturally do if given the scenario you've placed them in. In other words, whatever choice they made in your first go-round with them at that yellow light, they'd do something else now that they (and you, as the writer) have had the chance to fully inhabit the story as it developed.

Those are breadcrumbs you dropped for your future self—you know, the one on the other side of the completed first draft, who has the gift of hindsight on the story as it turned out to be at the end—to find and follow. In my own writing, these crumbs start appearing by the end of the first third, or just around the middle, as I'm really getting to know my story, and I carry them the rest of the way.

If you're wondering, yes, breadcrumbs will be there for you too. I truly believe that the answers to what your story needs—what opportunities are present in it but just not yet expressed or developed, what possibilities you have for your revision—are already on the page, somewhere in your story. Not in complete form, perhaps. But that writer brain you have, that plumbs your memories and presents you with ideas, has dropped crumbs onto your pages. You may not be aware of it, but the editor side (or perhaps a second set of eyes) will pick up on them.

Don't be afraid if the crumbs you see strewn about are things you wrote that perhaps you weren't even conscious of. You said what you felt, not what you thought you were going to say. You said the quiet part out loud, through a character or a sequence. And now it's staring at you.

Those early-to-mid-draft changes and course corrections have a way of reverberating through your whole story. Not just from where you make that change on to the end, but the beginning as well. One of the truest and most relatable adages about writing addresses this: the last page you'll write is the first page of the story. You don't always know where the right place to begin your story is until you've reached the end. Only then does it become clear where it ought to start.

Now's the time to go back to the beginning, during this pass, with those midwork corrections in mind. Is there something at the beginning that has now been influenced by that change? If so, the "needlework" you want to do here begins early. Take that change in the character, or in the story, or the sequence of events, and begin to thread it back through the story to the end. It may not influence each and every section or scene, but once you know how the character or story has evolved, you'll be able to go through the chart we made and identify where those threads need to be. Which leads us to…

THE PURPOSE PASS

Based upon your first, high-level pass, as well as the charting you did and, most likely, your actual writing on the first draft, you're probably aware of at least one or two issues. You know them when you feel them: something about the manuscript as written nags at you. It keeps you up at night. It leaves you with an uncertain feeling, like "Is that really working? Is that really believable? Is that really what the character would do? Is that boring? Does it feel like a stretch? Do I sense the momentum dragging right there?"

One gut feeling that is always an absolute tell for me: "Do I lose interest at this part? Did I find writing this section less interesting, involving, or important than the other sections/characters?"

If your gut is sending you data like this, rejoice. This is exactly what revision is designed to detect and address. Now that you've gone through and charted the finished draft at a high level, it's time to make a list of these gut-level items that you can't quite crystallize but that absolutely linger for you.

Now, go back to the beginning and chart only the beginning, progress, and resolution of that character or issue. What do you see? Do you see the thing that you've been consciously or unconsciously focused on? Is it a pacing issue? A continuity issue (as in, the shift in that character or issue from scene to scene isn't consistent, or not well handled, or the transition from one to the next doesn't feel smooth)? Or is it more substantive? You'll want to refer back to the high-level questions to see if they offer guidance:

- *Do I need to cut any scenes or characters?*
- *Do I need to add any scenes or characters?*
- *Do I need to change any scenes or characters?*

With that information from the chart of this character or issue, revise just that, and then integrate those revised scenes into the book.

If you still can't quite put your finger on the issue after these approaches to studying and determining it, don't worry. Set it aside and come back to it, or save that discrete issue for an outside reader (here I am!).

Let's move closer still.

THE SCENE EDITS PASS

By now you've charted out the course of the story and the characters. You've added new scenes and revised existing scenes according to general thoughts about pacing, flow, and to address those nagging issues that emerged to this point. Now, let's break that chart down a bit more. Starting with the first scene on to the end, let's revisit those trusty two questions. Ask them about each scene.

- *What do I know?*
- *How do I know it?*

Additionally, ask these questions, then answer them all:

- *What are the characters doing?*
- *Why are they doing it?*
- *What is happening to them?*
- *Why is it happening?*
- *What happens next because of all this?*

What you're looking for in this pass is how each scene moves the story to the next scene, how those scenes move the characters chronologically, but also thematically. Are you writing the story of one woman's long journey from an inward existence to the courage to express herself? Is she rising through the ranks of a particularly difficult entity (military, police, law firm, the sciences, etc.) with her past in pursuit, in the form of a secret, a stalker, a jealous rival, etc.? It's actually fun to come up with hypothetical variations, by the way. They're endless, as we learned from our initial writing exercises (why isn't she stopping at the yellow light?).

Such evolutions of story, character, or conflict will be the purpose around which this pass through your work is constructed. Chart the character/theme/plot's course from chapter to chapter and scene to scene. How do they change, and how gradually/abruptly? How believably? Are there leaps that you sense wouldn't strike readers as valid or earned? Are those changes in synch with the world around them? Or does it feel as though the issue/character you're focused on is actually on a wholly separate course from the story in chief? Is that intended? Is it the best way? Or does it need to be addressed?

Based upon the information you glean from this pass, go ahead and revise those issues as, and where, they arise.

Now what?

READ!

Read it from beginning to end. It feels like a new book, doesn't it?

Keep notes of anything you encounter that feels a bit off, underdeveloped, or just in need of attention. Then go on back to the breadcrumb and/or purpose pass with those issues in mind.

This is revision. Doing a revision is like taking a series of walk-throughs in the house you've built to live in. First, you walk through to get the lay of the place. Its rooms, its views. Then you come back over and over because you want to inspect the crown molding, the locks on the doors, how fast and hot the bath water is. And on and on, down to the small details with each successive visit. That's when you know you've truly inhabited this story of yours, right down to the smallest details.

THE COPY EDIT PASS

We're getting down to those details we talked about—sentence structure, word choice, syntax, errors of tense or voice. One of the most common changes made at this juncture—certainly for me—is locating and revising the word that shouldn't be there but is, and the word that should be there but isn't. Have you ever had the experience of reading something and throwing a word into the sentence that isn't there? Or skipping over a word because it somehow felt awkward to say, or just because the sentence felt better—better suited to the emotion of the sentence, better fit with the person saying it—without that word in it? Have you ever paused mid-sentence, your mind hovering over the next thing to say because what's on the page just doesn't quite fit what you think should be there?

You were revising on the fly. When you read through your writing, that word you add that isn't there, is popping up because it ought to be there. The word you omit needs to be cut. That's a truly effective brand of copyediting.

Another helpful tool to use is word search. Any writing program will have it, and it's helpful in locating and reducing, or eliminating altogether, those words you suspect you rely on far too much.

During this pass, be on the lookout for that bane of every editor's existence: overuse of adverbs. Over-reliance on adverbs can lead to cluttered writing and redundant sentences that don't need them. Often the adverbs mean the same as the verb and just aren't necessary. Strong, compelling dialogue should use strong verbs rather than "-ly" adverbs, and nowhere is this more true that the undisputed champion of all overused adverb situations: any adverb modifying the verb *said*.

"I'm leaving," he said angrily.

"Oh really?" she said sarcastically.

"Yes, really," he responded acidly.

Get the idea? Dedicate at least one such pass to every line of dialogue. If you find these little modifiers lurking around "said" or "replied" or "cried," ask yourself if you really need them. Can the dialogue be strengthened to convey what you're trying to get across without the adverb clogging it up?

WORD SEARCH

If you suspect you're relying too much on a certain word, this is a quick way to get a feel for just how reliant you are. Do a search for that word. How many times does it pop up, out of the number of pages you have?

This issue can crop up around motifs (the distinctive idea or theme of the story, a recurrent symbol). If you sense, at this point in the revision process, that perhaps you hit that symbol a bit too often, search it out (i.e., "green light" for Gatsby). Place quotes around the motif if it's a phrase you're worried about, and then just like a word search, see how many times it comes up. Make liberal use of a thesaurus to substitute different, better word choices.

SPELLCHECK

Now you're getting to the really granular, almost-done stuff. Before you release your manuscript to the wild world, you certainly want to catch as many spelling errors as possible. Turning in a piece that has misspellings will give your writing an amateurish feel that, after all your hard work, it doesn't deserve!

Your writing program's spellcheck function is a simple one, but what about contextual spelling errors? You know the culprits. You meant "their," but you typed "there." In describing a window, you intended to say "pane" but it came out "pain" on the page. Spellcheck won't catch those. They aren't misspelled; they're just contextually wrong. Moreover, those sorts of errors are exactly the kind that your brain will often miss when you proofread.

What to do?

Try this: read it backward.

No, you funny person, that doesn't mean you try reading it while turning around. It means you start at the end—of the story, or the chapter, or the page—and then read each word, right to left. You're going backwards through your sentences, and because that's odd as far as your brain, eyes and usual method of reading goes, you'll automatically slow down and consider each word not as part of a sentence, but as its own little entity. You'll catch far more errors that way.

ACCURACY CHECK/LAST MINUTE RESEARCH
Why so late?

I presume that by now, the big-picture research is well out of the way. You know the contours of the world you've set your story in, whether real or wholly imagined. That was done a while back. No, this is where you fill in those blanks you left. There are bound to be a few. You get to a moment in the story and you're on a roll, so you leave a street name blank, or you dash off a brief margin note to yourself (What was money called in that era? Was this a curse word back then? Could she do this in zero gravity?). Now it's time to go back to those blanks, do what research or thinking you might need to answer them, and fill 'em in.

Don't be afraid to find out that what you thought would go there doesn't fit. You were wrong; zero gravity does NOT work that way. Accept what you now know should go there, and then, like any other breadcrumb, thread it through wherever that issue came up. It may change a lot or just a little. All good—that's revision!

READ OUT LOUD
I can't stress enough how helpful reading out loud is to your understanding of the good parts of your story and identifying those parts that may need some additional attention. Hearing your words in real time—not at the speed we tend to move when reading silently—is frankly a transformative way of taking your work in. The rhythm and flow of the sentences, the grounding of the dialogue in reality, the words or turns of phrase that sound jarring for any number of reasons—too flowery, too stilted, too stiff, not believable that people would talk that way—all announce themselves in ways that they just don't when you read it to yourself. Carve out some space and time for yourself and do this. Try to do it across a period of a couple of hours to really dig in.

For all of these revision approaches and tips, remember: your goal is to find what can be made better. What might be even stronger, even more moving, even more vivid, if you change this or that. In other words, you're looking for the things that need fixing. This is NOT the same as self-criticism. Try not to get down on yourself as you find errors, or realize that something large needs to be rethought, or you find an inconsistency that "ought" to have been glaring, but you didn't see it. We all do this and more. Revision is not like turning your test in to your teacher and getting it back with the living hell marked off of it. Revision is every bit the writer working on their story, just like the first draft. That first draft is like opening the box and taking all the parts out, laying them side by side and making sure you emptied the box completely. Revision is where you put it together, where you help it take shape, and where you polish it to a high sheen.

Revision is writing, and if you've come this far, then remind yourself: only real writers do what you're doing.

THE FIRST TEN

As long as we're talking about revision, let me pass along some intel I've received on writers' panels and conferences from just about every agent I've ever encountered: the first ten pages of your book are, to state it plainly, make or break.

Now, I don't want you to feel pressured or anxious at that. But if you're writing to publish either traditionally or via self-publishing, this truth equally applies to the experience editors and readers will have. Those first ten pages are the territory in which a simple decision is made—should I keep going, or put this book down?

In the case of agents (and editors at publishing houses of every type and size), the fact of the matter is, they're impossibly overwhelmed. They have far, far more to read than they can reasonably get to. Assistants don't help; they're overwhelmed too! Agents receive hundreds of queries each week. They often skip synopses (because let's face it, even the most talented writers find synopses difficult to write—there's a reason why publishing houses pay copywriters to do the jacket copy for a book).

The first ten pages merit your attention precisely because it's where the attention of your intended audience, be it agents, editors, or readers, will be most keenly applied. We live in a Twitter world of reduced attention spans. While that doesn't necessarily mean there needs to be an explosion on page one, it does mean that the hook we spoke of earlier needs to be a sharp, engaging, and intriguing one. Ask yourself: what would make me want to turn the page to find out what happens next in this story?

There's an adage in publishing. "The first page sells this book. The last page sells the next one."

To further underscore the importance of a compelling opening, consider the top ten reasons agents (or editors) might stop reading and move on to the next manuscript:

- *Nothing happens.*
- *They've seen it before.*
- *There's no strong, distinctive voice telling the story.*
- *They're bored.*
- *They feel no connection with the characters.*
- *They can't tell what type of story it is.*
- *They don't care what happens next.*
- *The plot seems unbelievable or cliché.*
- *The dialogue doesn't sound like real people, or everyone sounds alike.*
- *Typos and grammar issues make the manuscript feel amateurish.*

Now, here are the top reasons they keep going:

- *Something happens (because you focused on your inciting incident).*
- *A strong voice (you can feel the character…because the author really knows them).*
- *A high level of craft is on display (because you revised it to a high sheen).*
- *The writer gains the reader's confidence (because you've established a vivid setting, distinctive characters, and put them in relatable and compelling situations).*
- *It's clear what sort of story it is.*
- *There's a market for it.*
- *The prose is concise and clear.*

Notice that a number of these are within your control; in fact, we worked on them together throughout this book! Some others—what the market seems to be going for, as an example—are not in our control, nor should you chase them. As we covered, it won't work, and you may make yourself unhappy by writing what you think may sell, not what compelled you to start in the first place. Stay true to your craft, to your idea, and to yourself.

NOTES ON MEMOIR

THE PRINCIPLES OF STRUCTURE AND REVISION that we've covered to this point can certainly apply to memoir. Though I'm no expert in the form, I'd like to suggest that there are certain dynamics the memoir writer should try to embrace as part of the experience they'll have writing it.

The first thing to embrace: In any recollected piece, there will be elements of fiction. Fictive tissue holds the piece together. That fact doesn't make your memoir a work of fiction.

Recall a conversation you had from several months ago, or a childhood memory of a birthday party, or the first argument you ever had with someone you love. I know, I can barely remember what I made for dinner last night. And that's the point: when we remember a conversation or a situation, our memory isn't a court reporter. It doesn't take down every word spoken, nor does it perfectly preserve every action, every sound or smell, every detail of where we were, what everyone wore, how everyone moved, and so on. We remember the broad strokes, the general idea. We remember the main things, and most importantly, we remember—we preserve—what we took away from that memory and how it's affected us over time. What we take away from conversations and moments tends to change, along with us. That's the fictive element of memory at work.

Think of it this way—are facts more important to the story you intend to write? If the answer is yes, then you may be writing an autobiography, and that will be dependent on research, interviews, the mining of your life and the lives of those who were around in each of your life's phases, who can provide firsthand accounts, photos, writings, etc. Autobiography is usually written in first person, and can be a bit more formal. It's obviously fact-based and is frequently structured chronologically.

If emotions are more front-and-center, then you're likely tackling a memoir. While memoir shares certain elements in common with autobiography—namely, the use of life experiences—memoir uses them to paint a larger theme of emotional resonance and truth. Memoirs play with memory. Some of the most compelling ones use that subjective view of "what happened" as a way of illustrating the memoirist's state of mind, view of the world, unique perspective, or transcendence of difficult, even traumatic circumstances.

The fictional tissue holding our memories in place, which bend and change over time? In autobiography, that can be a pitfall. In memoir, that can be an opportunity, to explore *how* you recall things. It's a chance for the writer to explore how the present life has put the past in a new context…or, perhaps, changed entirely how the past looks from out here.

Another thing a memoirist should try to embrace: Just because it happened—or happened to you—doesn't make it interesting.

The extraordinary memoirist Vivian Gornick once said, "What happened to the writer isn't what matters. What matters is the larger sense that the writer is able to make of what happened."

Remember that writers workshop I told you about? There was a writer whose work was critiqued, and it so happened that her own life was integrally tied to the story. When the criticism came down, it felt to her like a condemnation of her life and her choices. It felt personal, it wounded her deeply…and some portion of it was totally on target. Which part?

The story wasn't told in a very compelling way.

You may hear this sort of feedback whether you're writing in the fiction or memoir space, or something else (poetry, flash fiction, essay). Inevitably, some part of you *will* find its way into the piece. It will seem relatable, compelling, and vital to you, because it happened—literally, perhaps, or through a prism of maturity, sobriety, or an embrace of a truth you weren't ready at that time to face. It will seem, in the face of all these things, that it's told just as it should be. And so, this sort of feedback will be a cold shot, babe (all you sharp-eyed music fans know who I just quoted—DM me if you don't!).

What do you do with this sort of statement when it's made about your memoir? Your life, at least in terms of how it feels?

Apply the Grandma Rose theory, for starters. The Grandma Rose theory, you ask? It goes like this: A long, long time ago, my late grandmother Rose said something that had absolutely nothing whatsoever to do with writing. Forgive the cursing, but that was my grandma!

I forget what we were talking about, but in the middle of that conversation, she said, "If someone calls you an ass, they're very rude. If two people call you a bitch, you're probably an ass."

And thus was born the "Grandma Rose theory," aka some of the best writing advice I ever received.

If one person offers feedback on something that's not working, ok. Work with it if it resonates with you, or attribute it to one subjective reaction if it doesn't. But if more than one person starts referencing the same general issue, even if they're coming at it from different directions, now you have an issue to address and a decision to make. Essentially, you have data. Whatever you thought that character/situation/decision was communicating, turns out that it's not.

NOTES ON CRITICISM & REJECTION

IF YOU SEARCH "WRITERS AND REJECTION" or "writers and criticism" on the net, you'll emerge with a metric ton of results. "Famous writers on their worst rejections." "Five tips (or ten, or fifty) on dealing with rejection." There are whole books on the subject! I found one called *Don't Take It Personally*.

More platitudes have been written on the topic of writing and rejection than can be found on Pinterest and Instagram combined. I'm kidding...a little.

Rejection, criticism, whatever can be said of them, are always, always two things, no matter your outlook on them. First, they're inevitable for anyone who decides to write in a public-facing way. When you send out your manuscript to an agent, or thereafter to a publishing house, or to a magazine, or to a beta reader, there will inevitably be something among the responses you get that is grounded in some variation of "it's not for me." Every writer who seeks to be published is intimately familiar with the phrase "it's just not right for our list."

The second thing that is always true and will always *be* true, about rejections and criticism: it hurts. It feels personal. That feeling is there whether it's your first piece or your umpteenth.

And that's ok. In the words of my boxing trainer and sparring partner: "Yeah, it hurts, you're sucking wind. But did you die?"

Me: "No, but—"

Trainer: "Good. On to round two."

Having teased the platitude-y nature of available advice on this subject, I hope you'll forgive me if I say this: it really does only take one.

Have you ever read a book everyone was raving about, or went to a movie on the breathless recommendation of a friend, or listened to a band that's generating lots of buzz, and came away thinking, *I'm not seeing what the hype's about?* That doesn't mean they weren't good, even excellent, in craft, execution, or presentation. It's just that at that moment, occupying the same space as that piece of creativity, it didn't speak to you the way it might speak to someone else more attuned to that sort of thing.

Some of the most famous authors in history were rejected again and again before they found success. There are a lot of websites devoted to collecting their rejection letters, and it makes for stunning and occasionally really funny reading. So when you're working on finding literary representation and it's feeling hopeless, try to remind yourself that the best thing you can do for yourself is stay positive, even when the only person who seems to have your back is you. Just because one (or two, or forty) agents don't quite get you enough to offer representation doesn't mean another agent won't find your writing thrilling and just right for their list. With that said, if agents give you feedback, you should consider it—remember the Grandma Rose theory. The key is to know the difference between words of advice that can potentially open up ideas for your revision and words that basically translate into "it's not for me," which are relatively meaningless and certainly don't give you any guidance.

If you haven't labored over your story—I mean really bled over it, worked through it over and over, thinking about each character and story decision you made, revising and revising (which, as we know, is where the writing really lives)—then criticism or even rejection may be the right response to your piece. After all, you don't step into the ring until you've trained yourself for the moment. We all owe our writing the very best we can bring to it.

But if you've gone through the arduous task of working on your story until it's ready to be seen, and it STILL receives criticism or rejection, you'll likely deal with feelings of inadequacy, despair at anyone ever liking it, anger that they didn't see what you were trying to achieve, or envy of other writers who (at least this is how it strikes you in the moment of coping with the response you received) never have to deal with rejection or criticism. The feedback may feel personal—deeply so. You may tell yourself that it isn't intended that way, that it was meant to help you see where your writing can be improved upon, that the workshop, or agent, or publisher, or beta reader, are giving you their reaction to your story, and all such reactions are, as we noted above, subjective.

And yet.

Early in my writing career, I joined a writers workshop. Like most such workshops, we either wrote pieces specifically for the next session or we brought our works in progress (our novels, memoirs, etc.), and we'd read them aloud. In one such workshop, we distributed excerpts of the work at the end of one session, so everyone could read it for the next session and have their comments ready.

One of the participants in the workshop distributed an excerpt from her novel for the next session. I happened to know, from chatting with her, that the novel bore a close resemblance to a time in her life and a life decision she'd made in her youth. The excerpt she passed out was the moment in her novel where that decision is made, and the immediate consequence revealed. Suffice to say, the decision—in her life and in the novel—was a controversial one involving family and parenting.

The reaction to the excerpt, I suspect, mirrored the reaction she received in life. A few tried to understand it. A few tried to explore why it happened. The rest condemned it, and the writing of it. The writer running the workshop had to intervene because the comments were starting to get caustic and dismissive.

And the writer of the novel? She was deeply hurt, very upset, and discouraged to the point of giving up.

I learned a few lessons on navigating criticism and rejection from this episode.

First: take a moment and recognize yourself for the extraordinary courage it takes to write. All writers are familiar with the adage "write what you know." As we've seen, injecting your story with bits and pieces of yourself can certainly ease your way into your work, as descriptions of familiar places, shaped by your experiences with and within them, allow you to get into a flow of place-setting and evocation of the life of your characters in an intimate way. But, as I suspect you may now be seeing from the workshop incident, that way lies a potential hidden danger: the more you inject of yourself into your writing, the more susceptible you are to the unique wound that comes from the criticism or dismissal of your writing when it's *you* you're writing about. Your life, your realizations, your secrets, your reflection upon what's gone before and what's to come.

Here's the thing: don't let that stop you. "Write what you know?" If I may, allow me to suggest a more potent adage, that writers—no matter the genre, no matter the lightness of tone or far-flung (as in, this story has *nothing* to do with you) nature of your work—will come to know:

Write what you don't want anyone to know.

If you're truly writing, if you're digging into your story, your characters, their journeys...if you're really putting out all the sweat and tears on the page of your work, then the type of story doesn't matter; this will happen. You'll write a character, and perhaps they remind you of someone, and perhaps that in turn reminds you of your feelings toward them, or the dynamics of the relationship, or a thing that happened once, and there it will be, on the page: the truth you never said out loud. The feeling you didn't quite realize you had. The old anger, or lust, or regret, still there. The thing you didn't want anyone to know is now in your story, woven into the very thread of it, and it's a beating heart that demands that you leave it there.

And that means it's there to be reviewed, critiqued, even rejected. And that will hurt. No way around it.

So, the first thing I learned: when we put ourselves out there in our writing, we're on a high wire. We're stating our truth and taking our power, and yet we're extraordinarily vulnerable. Acknowledge that. We're human. We're writers. A shot at our work feels like a shot at us, whether that's what was intended or not.

"But did you die?"

No, we did not. The writer of the piece did not. All the rest of us who received criticism during the course of that workshop did not. You, when it happens (and it will), will not. Which was the second lesson I learned. Nurse the wound, scream about how lousy it feels, commiserate with writers and friends, and stand back up. We have work to do.

Another lesson: it so happened that the writer took a few of the notes she received (more on that below), rewrote the novel, and sent it back around to a few beta readers. The feedback was still mixed, but one person really got what she'd been trying to convey in the section she'd previously brought to the workshop. The reader got it as a device in the novel, if not in life. The author walked away feeling better about her decision and its execution.

I saw it for myself: it really does only take one.

Not everyone will get what you're trying to do. It may be that they don't see what you're going for, or appreciate the arcs of the story or its characters, because they're predisposed to dislike that sort of story. If that's the case, they aren't your audience, be they beta readers, prospective agents, or publishing houses. That's out of your control. On to the next, because it only takes one of them—one agent, one editor at a publisher—to see what it is that drove you to bleed, sweat and write what you've placed in front of them.

It may be, though, that they don't get it because something isn't working. Once you give yourself a bit of time to move past the sting of criticism, ask yourself, is there anything in that feedback that might be accurate? Is there something to learn? Buried in the "I didn't like" or "I don't think this part worked," might there be something that could make the story even stronger?

One of the more challenging aspects of receiving criticism is the inconsistency. Attend any writers workshop during a feedback session, and bear witness to the sheer confusion that is the range of reactions and suggestions the poor writer receives on the excerpt they shared. "I really wanted to see more of the CEO. She was the most interesting part of the piece."

"I really wanted to see way less of the CEO. I really disliked her and couldn't understand any of her choices."

"What were you going for with the CEO's choices in this section? I was confused."

"The CEO made a really great choice in that section. Keep it just as it is. Better, rewrite the story to show the consequences of that choice. Lose the rest."

"You need a flashback there to explain the CEO."

"You need to stay in the moment with the CEO."

What's the writer to do? Whose opinion counts? None of them? All of them?

This tug of war with the writer's emotions—not to mention the decisions they have to make on how, or even whether, to revise—is especially tough when the warring viewpoints come during the submission phases. There's a strong (to put it mildly) temptation to revise around the feedback of an agent who passes, but hold out hope either for a fresh look after the story is revised, or revise for an agent who passes definitively but has suggestions for how to make it better. Then along comes the next agent and the next, and behold: they have a different take. They love what the last agent hated and hated what they loved. The same can hold true when it comes to conflicting editorial feedback once an agent is submitting the manuscript to publishers.

Oy!

The key to taking criticism in is, of course, sorting through what may feel like rejection in order to find the parts that can help you with the big picture issue: get your writing in the best possible shape and get it where you want it to go—like your favorite literary journal, or the shelves of the world's bookstores.

Take a fresh look at that crossfire hypothetical I set out above, the one where the poor writer is receiving all sorts of conflicting feedback about the CEO. Different takes on the CEO. Different directions on the CEO. Keep the CEO. Ditch the CEO. Notice anything?

It's all about the CEO. In this hypothetical, the specific feedback isn't as telling as the fact that, regardless of the conflicting directions, there's something about the CEO character that's not communicating in the way the author intended. And that's incredibly valuable as data to you, the writer. That data has now brought you to a decision point.

The particulars may differ, but the theme of this hypothetical feedback is entirely consistent. Something about the way the CEO character is written, and/or the scenes she appears in, and/or the way the story shapes itself and progresses around and because of her, isn't communicating the way the author intended. Different readers are consuming and reacting to that aspect in different ways, but the issue for the writer is plain: all these pieces of feedback tell me that the character and her place in the story is taking them in different directions. Is that what I intended? Did I mean to create a character, an arc for her, and the story's motion around and because of her, so that she'd hit different people different ways? Stop them in their tracks so they would have to deal with her before moving on to the story again? Is that what I meant to happen?

To be sure, the answer may be "yes." Perhaps your goal with the piece was to create a character who confounds or confuses. If that's the case, your decision point is this: now you know that the character is halting readers. It's hitting different readers differently. Those readers may be workshop peers, but (if this is your goal for the story) at some point they'll be agents and editors. How will you feel when they're the ones reacting like this?

If the answer is "I'll feel fine because that's the story I set out to tell," then your decision is made: the character stays as they are.

If, however, you didn't realize the character would strike readers that way, you have a different decision point. You need to revise.

The takeaway: all writing, from choice of words to where the story ends to what paths the characters travel (along the route you outlined, or breaking off as they develop) is a decision you as the writer make. You listen to your story as it grows through the first draft and through all the revisions, but ultimately the choices are yours alone.

THE QUIET

Something all writers know: the quiet. Maybe it's the quiet while you wait for a reader to let you know what they think of your manuscript. Or for an agent you admire to tell you whether they believe in what you've written, enough to take you on. Trust me, there will be times when you send out queries and it feels like you've tossed them down a deep dark hole, never to be heard from again. Or maybe it's the quiet while an editor considers that thing you worked for years to bring out of yourself, into the world. Or the quiet that settles in while you revise.

You know, the quiet where you wonder if it'll happen.

Listen:

Believe in yourself the way you did when that daunting idea—the one you weren't sure you were good enough to pull off—refused to leave you. Remember what you did? You said "I can do this." Believe in yourself like that, because that's how I believe in you. Believe that someone else will believe in you too. When those quiet moments come where you wonder whether this is worth it, whether you can do it, whether you ought to give up, reach out to me. Even if we don't know each other, I know this about you: you're a writer. Tell me what you wrote, and I'll tell you what you achieved by writing it.

We all know that quiet. It's ok. Quiet is just the absence of sound, but that's how you wrote in the first place. In quiet. See? Great things come from quiet. You got this.

Hang in there, and know that I'm here for you and will help you navigate the bumps along the way. Hey, those bumps will be great material for your acknowledgements page when you get published!

CONCLUSION

YOU DID IT!

If you've been writing alongside the chapters of this book, take this moment to congratulate and be truly proud of yourself – you're well on the way to a complete, revised, and ready-to-be-seen book of your own! May I say, I'm proud of you. We all dream of doing things, but it takes fearlessness, dedication, and confidence in the worthiness of your own voice to get here, the end of this book and its many (hopefully fun and informative) exercises. Writing is, as you've no doubt noticed, a solitary undertaking. While being alone on your journey doesn't have to mean you're lonely, there are times in all writers' lives when we feel like we're the only ones who believe in the stories we're trying to tell.

I hope you know that your writing and all it entails – starting, finishing, revising, polishing – has found a home right here.

Let's consider what you accomplished, shall we?

We overcame one of the biggest hurdles – generating an idea – with some exercises designed to warm up our writerly muscles. We built those ideas out with research – and the always helpful question, *why?* We examined story structure and considered different ways that structure can be designed. We tackled point of view, character arc, and conflict types, and we focused in on setting and making it as vivid and alive as your characters.

From there we moved to the outline phase, where we discussed some strategies you can use to map out your story from A to Z, with room for creative digression, experimentation, and fun with your story's many possibilities. We talked about issues all writers experience at one point or another on their journey –Criticism, writer's block, rejection, and even the dreaded wait –and we went over some thoughts on how to deal with them when they do crop up. We tackled revision strategies and went over ideas on how to sift through competing choices to find the best ones for your work.

That's a lot! But now you have a roadmap of your own to spark, inspire, and guide you. And though you've finished this book, I'm still here for you! Please do come find me and my private Facebook Group, The Write Formula, and join our community! I'm always there to talk writing, from inspiration to getting through those inevitable challenges.

Finally, a heartfelt thank you…to you! I'm grateful to be a part of your writing journey, and I really can't wait to read your story!

ACKNOWLEDGEMENTS

I'm forever grateful to my wife and partner in crime Nina, for her unwavering belief in me and her understanding when writing takes me away. To my extraordinary daughters Ariel and Kavanna – you are inspirational and amazing every day.

I feel so fortunate to have a wonderfully supportive, loving literary community around me. Whether through my novels, my Write Formula group, or my reading series, Roar Shack, I feel incredibly lucky to be in the company of deeply talented, empathetic, and joyful fellow authors or all kinds. A very special thank you to Aruni Wijesinghe, Toni Ann Johnson, Sandra Hunter, Kate Maruyama, and the entire Los Angeles literary community. You are family.

To my forever mentor and friend Susan Taylor Chehak, who taught me above all else that there is room for all who want to put their words into the world, if they're willing to work at it. Thank you for all you've done for me and for others.

To my English teacher Gloria Luxenberg, who once told a little boy that he could write. You inspired a lifetime, my friend.

And finally, to you and to all writers out there – I've learned so much from each of you about dedication, about community, and about the extraordinary act of putting down the words we all carry. Thank you.

INDEX

A
Action piece, 27
Action-based stories, 23
Adult fiction, 24
Antagonist, 49, 91
Aristotle, 73
Autobiography, 113, 114

B
Background event, 102
Backstory, 13, 34, 49, 53, 64, 84
Becket, Samuel, 7
Behind the Beautiful Forevers, 13
Beta reader, 89, 96, 117, 118
Blueprint method, 8, 78, 80, 99
Boo, Katherine, 13

C
Cameron, James, 30
Cameron, Julia Margaret, 11
Character arc, 13, 21, 23, 52, 53, 92, 100, 125
Character development, 47, 48, 84
Character goal, 22
Character identifiers, 41
Character traits, 47
Character world, 23, 27
Chronological chart, 102
Chronological progression, 84
Chronological storyline, 31
Claustrophobic view, 34
Cliché, 111
Climactic confrontation, 28, 29
Completion fear, 99
Complication, 27
Composite of people, 6
Confessions of Max Tivoli, The, 35
Conflict, 25, 74, 75, 79, 84
    Character arc, 125
    Character indentifiers, 42
    Development, 21

Evolution, 106
Ideas, 4, 23
Identifying, 74
Main, 73
Main character, 85
Outcome, 60, 61
Relevance, 86
Resolution, 28, 58
Revelation, 48
Set in motion, 91
Story arc, 60
Story momentum, 57
Type, 57, 58
Unavoidable, 86
Consequences, 23, 24, 25, 26, 33, 59, 73, 74, 85, 91, 121
Crime fiction, 7, 12, 23
Crisis, 27, 50, 75
Critical information, 84
Criticism, 109, 114, 117, 118, 119, 120, 121, 125
Cultural legacy, 18

D
Dialogue, 2, 15, 48, 66, 71, 84, 95, 107, 108, 109, 111
Distinctive voice, 111
Draft stage, 101

E
Enter the Dragon, 66, 83, 88
Epiphany, 28
Exercises
    Character arc, 92
    Characters, 41, 42, 43, 48, 50
    Flash, 60
    Freewriting, 2
    Plot, 78
    POV, 37
    Scene creation, 72, 73
    Setting, 65

Story, 15, 18
Story ideas, 3, 4, 9
Story momentum, 51
Story structure, 26, 27, 28, 29, 30, 31
Exposition, 22, 26, 73, 77, 99
External action, 34

F
Fictive element of memory, 113
First act, 22, 23, 24, 27, 28
First draft, 8, 12, 22, 35, 89, 95, 96, 97, 99, 101, 102, 104, 110, 122
  Writing, 105
Firsthand accounts, 113
First-person narrator, 24
First-person story, 33
Fitzgerald, F Scott, 25, 30
Flash fiction, 1, 4, 114
Flashback, 29, 33, 36, 78, 79, 83, 84, 85, 86, 87, 88, 121
Flypaper effect, 42
Flystrip effect, 1, 6
Foreshadow, 27, 79
Freewriting, 1, 2
Freytag pyramid, 73
Futuristic fiction, 7

G
Genre fiction, 7
Getty Museum, 11, 16, 17
Great Gatsby, The, 24, 25, 30, 64, 66, 67, 108
Greer, Andrew Sean, 35

H
Happenstance, 3
High level pass, 102 Hook, 22, 23, 110
Horror fiction, 7, 23

I
Imposter syndrome, 89
Inciting incident, 22, 23, 24, 25, 26, 27, 28, 111

Inner world events, 42
Interior life, 47
Internal action, 34
Internal conflict, 53, 57
Interview, 113

J
Jaws, 23, 24, 27, 28
Journalism, 13

K
Key conflict, 54
King, Stephen, 6

L
LGBTQIA, 7
Literary fiction, 7, 8, 24, 74, 118, 121
Live write, 2
Luminist, The, 11, 16, 17, 42

M
Main action, 23, 27
Main character, 12, 26, 35, 36, 43, 45, 75
  Conflict, 26, 59, 85
  Dilemma, 54
  Enter the Dragon, 83
  Exercise, 12, 17
  Journey, 22
  Night Language, The, 36, 37, 97
  Outline, 86
  Point of no return, 28
  Shortcomings, 54
  Strengths, 27
  Traits, 13
Main Plot, 102
Manuscript, 96, 101, 102, 105, 108, 111, 117, 121, 122
Memoir, 1, 5, 6, 8, 71, 74, 83, 95, 113, 114
Memoirist, 114
Mentor, 8
MFA, 73
Moment of truth, 28, 59

Monologue, 33, 36, 37, 47, 84
Morality, 48
Mystery, 7
Mystery fiction, 23

N
Narrative pace, 27
Narrative summary, 83, 84, 86
Narrative voice, 25, 35
Narrator, 24, 33, 34, 84, 88
Night Language, The, 12, 17, 36, 37, 97

O
Oliver Twist, 24
Opening, 1, 13, 15, 25, 83, 110, 111
Out a scene, 48
Outer world events, 42
Outline, 72, 79
    Characters, 74, 85
    Completed, 60
    Creation, 99
    Framework, 72
    Freewriting, 1
    Revivion, 8
    Story movement, 75
    Story structure, 78
Outline phase, 125
Outward behavior, 47

P
Pacing, 84, 105
Parallel storylines, 30
Period romance, 7
Personality trait, 3
Perspective, 30, 33, 34, 35, 37, 79, 90, 114
    First person, 33
    New, 30
    Third person, 34
Pinch point, 27, 28, 73, 77
Plot, 79, 91, 99
    Arc, 13
    Building method, 11, 17
    Character development, 53, 59
    Conflict, 4
    Definition, 77
    Generation, 6
    Leap, 103, 106
    POV, 37
    Rewrite, 101
    Scene creating, 71, 72
    Story momentum, 60
    Structure, 22, 23, 27
    Unbelievable, 111
    Writer block, 85
    Writers, 84
Plot arc, 34, 79
Plot point, 22, 23, 27, 47, 68, 79, 85, 100
Plot-driven, 7
Plotlines, 30, 31, 34
Point of no return, 28
Point of View, 33, 35, 36, 37, 38, 43, 48, 58, 79, 86, 88
    First person, 33, 34, 35, 36, 37, 50, 73, 79, 113
    Impact, 85
    Second person, 35
    Third person, 34
POV. See Point of View
Primary conflict, 50
Prompt, 2, 3, 4, 65
Protagonist, 49, 91
Publishing house, 117

R
Read out loud, 109
Reading experience, 8, 79
Reading pace, 5
Real person, 6
Recollected piece, 113
Rejection, 117, 118, 119, 121, 125
Relevance, 86
Research
    Accuracy, 109
    Big picture, 15, 109
    Books and movies, 15
    Character identifiers, 42, 43
    Focused, 12
    General, 14

Ideas, 125
Importance, 13
Letters and records, 16
Memoir, 113
Opportunities, 14
Photos and art, 17, 18
Process, 14, 50
Scene creation, 71
Story, 13, 14
Story structure, 21, 30
The Story, 12
Valid form, 14
Research types, 14
Revision, 4, 8, 14, 29, 37, 47, 89, 96, 97, 98, 99, 100, 101, 102, 104, 105, 107, 108, 109, 110, 113, 118, 125
Rhythm, 109
Rising action, 27, 73, 74
Rising conflict, 27

S
Second-act, 22, 23, 27
Second-person narrative, 35
Secondary characters, 13, 43
Self-conflict, 59
Sentence flow, 96
Sentence structure, 102, 107
Series of events, 27
Setting, 64, 125
    Creation, 63, 64, 65, 66, 67
    Criticism, 119
    Idea, 11
    Plot blueprint, 79, 80
    Research, 15, 16
    Rewriting, 98, 101
    Scene creation, 71
    Story structure, 21, 22, 25
    Vivid, 111
    Writer block, 83
Short story, 1, 5, 6, 8, 35, 71, 87, 95
Spellcheck, 95, 108
Spielberg, Steven, 23
Star Wars, 27
Story arc, 23, 43, 52, 92

Story collection, 95
Story creation, 4
Story midpoint, 28, 73, 74
Story outline, 71
Story premise, 71
Story structure, 21, 22, 23, 24, 29, 30, 83, 96, 98, 113, 125
    Freewriting, 1
    Outline, 78
Structure of revelation, 77
Styron, William, 59
Subplot, 102
Subtext rules, 47
Supporting characters, 13, 75, 103

T
Tension, 37, 38, 48, 73, 84
Third act, 28, 29
Three-act arc, 21
Thriller fiction, 7, 12, 23, 35
Timeframe, 11, 86
Timeline, 28, 29, 43
Titanic, 30
Trauma, 49, 75
Trigger, 88
Turning point, 50, 85

U/V
Unresolved event, 6
Verb tense, 37, 86

W
Word choice, 102, 107
Work of fiction, 113
Worsening. See Rising action
Writer block, 83, 88, 89, 125
Writing exercises, 106

Y
Yellow Light Game, 3, 50, 92

ABOUT THE AUTHOR

DAVID ROCKLIN is the author of two novels, *The Luminist* (published in the U.S and Italy) and *The Night Language*, the recipient of a Foreword award. He is the creator and host of The Write Formula writer's retreat in Idyllwild, CA. He also hosts and curates Roar Shack, a popular monthly reading series based in Los Angeles. The series is in its tenth year.

www.ingramcontent.com/pod-product-compliance
Lightning Source LLC
Chambersburg PA
CBHW061209070526
44583CB00025B/3170